PENGUIN BOOKS

BLUE GRIT

Laura Flanders hosts *RadioNation,* heard nationally on the Air America Radio network and on public radio. She is the author of *Bushwomen: Tales of a Cynical Species; Real Majority, Media Minority: The Cost of Sidelining Women in Reporting;* and the editor of *The W Effect: Sexual Politics in the Bush Years and Beyond.* A National Institute "fellow," Flanders lives in New York City. For more information, please visit www.lauraflanders.com.

Blue Grit

Making Impossible, Improbable,
and Inspirational Political Change
in America

Laura Flanders

PENGUIN BOOKS

PENGUIN BOOKS

Published by the Penguin Group

Penguin Group (USA) Inc., 375 Hudson Street, New York, New York 10014, U.S.A.
Penguin Group (Canada), 90 Eglinton Avenue East, Suite 700, Toronto,
Ontario, Canada M4P 2Y3 (a division of Pearson Penguin Canada Inc.)
Penguin Books Ltd, 80 Strand, London WC2R 0RL, England
Penguin Ireland, 25 St Stephen's Green, Dublin 2, Ireland (a division of Penguin Books Ltd)
Penguin Group (Australia), 250 Camberwell Road, Camberwell,
Victoria 3124, Australia (a division of Pearson Australia Group Pty Ltd)
Penguin Books India Pvt Ltd, 11 Community Centre,
Panchsheel Park, New Delhi – 110 017, India
Penguin Group (NZ), 67 Apollo Drive, Rosedale, North Shore 0632,
New Zealand (a division of Pearson New Zealand Ltd)
Penguin Books (South Africa) (Pty) Ltd, 24 Sturdee Avenue,
Rosebank, Johannesburg 2196, South Africa

Penguin Books Ltd, Registered Offices: 80 Strand, London WC2R 0RL, England

First published in the United States of America by The Penguin Press,
a member of Penguin Group (USA) Inc. 2007
Published in Penguin Books 2008

1   3   5   7   9   10   8   6   4   2

Grateful acknowledgment is made for permission to reprint
excerpts from the following copyrighted works:
Quote by Brian Greene. Used by permission of Brian Greene.
"On the Night of November 3, 1992" from *Affirmative Acts: Political Essays by June Jordan*
(Anchor Books, 1998). Copyright © 1998 by June Jordan. Reprinted by permission
of the June M. Jordan Literary Estate Trust.
"The Low Road" from *The Moon Is Always Female* by Marge Piercy. Copyright © 1980 by
Marge Piercy. Used by permission of Alfred A. Knopf, a division of Random House, Inc.
Asphalt by Carl Hancock Rux (Atria Books, 2004). Copyright © by Carl Hancock Rux.
Used by permission of the author.

THE LIBRARY OF CONGRESS HAS CATALOGED THE HARDCOVER EDITION AS FOLLOWS:
Flanders, Laura.
Blue grit : true Democrats take back politics from the politicians / by Laura Flanders.
p.   cm.
Includes bibliographical references and index.
ISBN 978-1-59420-113-4 (hc.)
ISBN 978-0-14-311322-5 (pbk.)
1. Democratic Party (U.S.)   2. Liberalism—United States.   3. United States—Politics and
government—2001–   I. Title.
JK2316.F56 2007
324.2736—dc22   2006035347

Printed in the United States of America
Designed by Mary Sarah Quinn

Dedicated to June Jordan (1936–2002),
who wrote:

And because revolution always takes place on the
basis of great hope and rising expectations, I am
not too worried about the future. One way or
another a whole lotta change is gonna come.
Through happiness realized or through and
beyond the pain of betrayal, we will become
the beneficiaries of our faith.

And even without revolution, we will prevail
because we have proven to the world, and to
ourselves, that we are not "fringe elements" or
"special interest groups" or so-called "minorities."
Without us there is no legitimate majority: we are
the mainstream. We have become the "people."

And let our elected leadership beware the awesome
possible wrath of a mighty, multifoliate, and
faithful people whose deepest hopes have been
rekindled and whose needs have not been met.

From "On the Night of November 3, 1992,"
in *Affirmative Acts: Political Essays*

Contents

Blue Grit

Foreword: Neo-Conned

The story of the Bush administration is one of a group of con men who led the United States, against the will of its people, into a disastrous war. It is, as we also know, the story of an administration beholden to corporate interests and not the public interest; an administration out of touch with what matters most to most Americans. It succeeded not only in dragging a nation into war, but into conning those who disagreed with it into believing they were out of touch, or worse, out of alternatives.

But there's another story, one that we don't hear much about, the story of what the brave and brilliant journalist Laura Flanders calls Blue Grit. That is the story of progressive change makers across the United States who prove that there are alternatives to the status quo, regardless of the assertions of the Bush administration and all too many Democrats. Flanders brings us stories of Blue Grit Americans who are waging exactly the kind of campaigns the mainstream media and their pet politicians tell us are impossible. And they're winning.

In so doing, Blue Grit offers an antidote to an insidious poison that pollutes our body politic, namely, the idea that we suffer a lack of ideas. I don't believe the problem is a lack of ideas. I think we're swimming in ideas: universal health care; living wages; co-operatives; participatory democracy; public services that are account-able to the people who use them; food, medicine, and shelter as human rights. These aren't new ideas. They're enshrined in the UN declara-tion. And I think most of us still believe in them.

The real problem is confidence, our confidence, the confidence of people who want to build another world, a more dignified, more sus-tainable world. Fed an endless diet of discouragement from the media and disparaged even by our supposed leaders, we come to lack the strength of our convictions, and the guts to back up our ideas with enough muscle movement to scare our elites.

"The best lack all conviction," Yeats wrote, "while the worst are full of passionate intensity." Think about it. What is wrong with us? Where is *our* passionate intensity?

I believe that what's at the root of our crisis of confidence, what drains us of our conviction at crucial moments when we are tested, is a dangerous, often unquestioned notion: the idea that our ideas have al-ready been tried and found wanting. It is this that keeps us from build-ing the alternatives that we deserve and long for and that the world needs so desperately—like a health-care system that doesn't sicken us when we see it portrayed on film, like a mass effort to rebuild New Orleans without treating a shameful human tragedy like an opportu-nity for rapid profit-making for politically connected contractors, like strengthening our infrastructure so we have bridges that don't collapse and subways that don't flood when it rains. At the root of our lack of po-litical confidence is the idea, repeated over and over again, that pro-gressive ideas have already been tried and failed. We hear it so much that too many of us have accepted it. So we pose our alternatives tenta-tively, almost apologetically. "Is another world possible?" we ask.

What's exciting about *Blue Grit* is that it has the power to give us guts. Through reporting on what's actually happening around the United States, and what lies beneath some of the political victories claimed by Democrats, Flanders challenges the dominant narrative of our time—the narrative of the intellectual and ideological failure of everyone but the super-capitalist right.

Blue Grit is a gift because we who say we believe in this other world need to know that we are not losers. We did not lose the battle of ideas. We were not outsmarted, and we were not out-argued. Around the world, progressives have been up against brutal forces. Sometimes those forces were crushed by army tanks, and sometimes they were crushed by think tanks (and by think tanks, I mean the people who are paid to think by the makers of tanks). Understanding that we never lost the battle of ideas, that we only lost a series of dirty wars, is key to building the confidence that we lack, to igniting the passionate intensity that we need.

Naomi Klein

Introduction

Blue Grit is a book of good news for grim times. It's not a feel-good book—it's a wise-up book, a challenge to all those who advise the Democratic Party to get tougher militarily, quote more scripture, cut social spending, and hush those pesky voices at the margins who raise awkward questions about peace and social justice. For those who believe that progressive change is impossible in the USA, it argues that the opposite is true: Americans are scoring progressive victories, even in some of the most conservative parts of the country. As they look toward 2008, the leaders of the Democratic Party could learn from those victories, if they were inclined to learn. The question is, does the party want to learn from blue voters with grit—or does it not?

Every week, people call in to *RadioNation,* the show that I host on Air America Radio. My listeners, everyday people, phone from across the country to talk about their lives, their politics, and their politicians. I hear their frustrations: how impossible it seems to create positive change that will shift people in power, and how fed up they are with their supposed leaders' lack of spine. But *RadioNation* has made a habit of airing the views of another group as well—people who are making change by taking power into their own hands, doing exactly those things that the political establishment says can't be done. Things like getting elected (twice) to be mayor of the largest city in the "reddest" state in the union, being pro–gay marriage, proenvironmentalist, and antiwar. Or running for office—and winning—as an out lesbian in Boise, Idaho, or a former welfare recipient in Helena, Montana (with four kids under eighteen in tow). I've heard from people who have organized the supposedly unorganizable—alienated young people, poor people, and marginalized immigrants—to protest, and even to take power, by getting smart about elections and running for office. *Blue Grit* tells those stories.

I do not predict who will win in 2008, but I do argue that no national party, least of all the Democratic Party, can survive by trying to flee its own base. It's not what Republicans have done. They've gone out of their way to cater to those at their flanks (right-wing Christians and anti-tax groups, among others). Those on the Democratic side, by contrast, keep their distance from their voters' movements. Throughout the 1990s the party did its best to ignore the fair trade movement, which grew up after the World Trade Organization protests in Seattle. When thousands of disproportionately Democratic voters marched against the invasion of Iraq in February 2003, few elected Democrats were in their ranks. It took three years for Democrats to even begin to catch up with their own voters on the need to withdraw U.S. troops from Iraq.

Many dismiss what happens on the margins. I say they're wrong—the margins are where the action is, where the hard work of winning majorities takes place, and where true democracy is most in evidence. In *Blue Grit*, I'll argue that a rumble of real change is rising and everybody who cares about Democracy—big or little *d*—needs to listen up.

I'll admit it, the mood at the nation's new liberal talk-radio network was bleak on election night 2004. Described in broad strokes, Air America's listeners—an attentive and engaged bunch—are overwhelmingly Democrats. Air America hosts, including Al Franken, Randi Rhodes, and Janeane Garofalo, dedicated themselves after the network's birth to rallying troops for a John Kerry victory. Judging from the calls I received over the year leading up to the election, Air America Radio's audience included many who had become politically active for the first time in that election season. They had raised money, staffed phone banks, even left their homes to run campaigns and knock on faraway strangers' doors—if not for Kerry, then to oust a deadly and disastrous president, George W. Bush. Probably no national media audience more closely reflected rank-and-file Democratic voters' dreads and desires than Air America Radio's listeners.

As I walked to work at about seven P.M. on Election Day, I listened to Al Franken broadcast live from Kerry headquarters. The unofficial word from "Kerry's people" was that the election was in the bag. I passed Union Square, the kick-off spot for spirited marches on the Republican National Convention just three months earlier, and remembered the last night of that convention, when Bush and Cheney's acceptance speeches had been interrupted three times by protestors from ACT UP and Codepink. An administration that promises the American people security and can't even protect the perimeter of its own event from guys fighting AIDS and antiwar women wearing pink nighties? It's got to be over, I thought then, and I wasn't alone.

Shortly after midnight, things were looking very different. Having pulled some invisible short straw, I was assigned the overnight shift, midnight to five A.M. Almost immediately my broadcast role changed from cheerleader of a hopeful and expectant liberal group to comforter of a doom-laden (but not dumbstruck) crowd. The insomniac listeners who called in to our toll-free number sounded like people who'd seen one too many "Vote or Die" posters. They had not anticipated voting *and* dying. In liberal America it seemed like the night of the politically living dead.

Not for nothing am I called an optiholic. While my listeners cursed their compatriots and talked about moving to Canada, my instinct was to try to cheer them up. Despite Kerry's loss, these facts were on my side: 2004 was a blockbuster election year. More voters cast ballots, more money was raised and spent, and more people participated in more election-related activities than in any election in years. Nearly 60 percent of eligible Americans cast a ballot (an increase of 6 percent). Out of 200 million eligible voters, 59 million had voted for George W. Bush, but 55 million had cast their ballot for Kerry, a guy whom the media had dubbed the most liberal man in the Senate.

Even as those states voted for George W. Bush, voters in Florida and Nevada approved ballot measures raising the minimum wage. The wage initiatives won majorities in every county, rural and urban, blue and red, rich and poor, in both states. Every one of the Democratic senators who voted against the Iraq war resolution won reelection by a healthy margin: Barbara Boxer (California), Russ Feingold (Wisconsin), Daniel Inouye (Hawaii), Patrick Leahy (Vermont), Barbara Mikulski (Maryland), Patti Murray (Washington), Ron Wyden (Oregon). As the months progressed, good news continued to turn up. Three months after an election that was supposedly decided on "moral values," Topeka voters rejected an anti–gay marriage city ordinance, and in Idaho, where Kerry scraped together just 30 percent of the vote, eight Republicans joined with Democrats in the state legislature to stop an anti–gay marriage constitutional amendment. There were reasons those victories were occurring but not reasons one could learn about on television.

It's old hat to say that media cover elections as if they were horse races. As the media critic Jim Naureckas points out, "The significance of that sort of coverage is that it makes it seem as if the only important players are the horses." Journalists do an excellent job of training our gaze away from the throng of people in the stands, down to the two politicians running around the track. Not even a week after the 2006 congressional elections (which by many accounts were a popular revolt) the Sunday morning TV news shows were at it again, talking not about what had just happened in the country, but about which politicians planned to run for president. Coverage like that obscures the public's role in events (hence all those *RadioNation* callers asking "What's the point?"). And rarely gives a second look to the electoral process.

When things go wrong, on the other hand, Democratic Party leaders, political consultants, and even the pundits seem to prefer to blame party foot soldiers first, and 2004 was a case in point. For the foot-soldier participants, after the disappointment came disparagement. Then *New Republic* editor Peter Beinart declared that the party's problem was the people in it: "Kerry was a flawed candidate," he wrote, "but [Kerry] was not the fundamental problem. The fundamental problem was the party's base." Bill Clinton's adviser and former deputy chief of staff Harold Ickes addressed a conference call of major Democratic donors, and (according to several participants) he blamed the party's defeat on gay marriage, abortion, and youth's failure to turn out. Jehmu Greene, executive director of Rock the Vote, was furious. Rock the Vote (which Greene says registered 1.4 million new voters in 2004) worked with an alliance of groups that did just what the party's consultants discouraged: they focused on young voters, eventually yielding the highest turnout since the voting age was lowered from twenty-one to eighteen in 1972. As many as 20.1 million Americans age eighteen to twenty-nine voted, up from 18 million in 2000, the biggest leap of any age demographic. Kerry utterly lacked juice on any youth-related issue, yet young voters (driven by African American and Hispanic young people, who make up a third of all eligible youth voters) handed the senator his only victory in any age group. Pollster Celinda Lake called it "one of the few successes in 2004." Still, only a quarter of young people voted. By focusing only on percentages (which stayed constant even as the number of voters jumped), Ickes skewed the data, missed the story, and dashed young hearts from coast to coast.

No wonder progressive Americans get discouraged. Jehmu Greene was thirty-two years old in 2004. She didn't give up, but she did step down from her position at Rock the Vote (membership had grown from 15,000 to 1 million in two years under her leadership), and she put on hold a political career that included working on-staff at the Democratic National Committee (DNC) and numerous campaigns, such as those of Clinton/Gore and Ann Richards. I found Greene a year later in Venice Beach, California, pondering what she wanted to do next. "They paid us no mind during the campaign. They'd only roll their eyes. Then when we do our bit and they lose again, the most powerful people in the party blame the youth for their mistakes?" said Greene, still smarting. "I went into the Democratic Party with an idealistic vision, but I'm cured." When Democrats cannibalize their own, who needs Karl Rove?

The Democratic establishment has a problem. It doesn't seem to like its foot soldiers much. After the 2004 election I heard no end of frustration about what one election organizer described as "a massive cultural divide between the party's people and those of us actually working, and living in the states." The Republicans, whom the Left casts as strictly top-down organizers, seem to be better at providing clear leadership from the top while also creating empowerment at the base, that organizer (who wished to remain anonymous so as not to offend his colleagues) told me. "The Democrats treat us with suspicion; there's a top-down feeling about their whole approach." With half the eligible population declining to vote, Democrats can hardly afford to turn off those who actually bother to participate.

Before we head back into another season at the presidential race track, *Blue Grit* calls for attention to the stands. Politicians, parties, and campaigns don't just "have" political positions, they "do" political acts: they conduct campaigns, raise money, set priorities, reach out to voters, treat their allies with (or without) respect. After a year spent interviewing organizers, activists, and participants within and outside the Democratic Party itself, it's clear to me that much about the way the Democrats have been "doing" politics simply stinks. Flying in last-minute once every four years and saying "Vote for us" and then flying out, leaving nothing behind—that way of doing politics may win elections from time to time, but it doesn't inspire; it alienates.

After the victories in 2006, there's a temptation to think the party's mojo is back, but it's not too late for a GOP hat trick in 2008. The same establishment media, party leaders, and well-paid campaign consultants that pass blame from top to bottom have another tendency as well, which is to shuttle credit from bottom to top. The Democratic Party has two presidential defeats behind it, the second in a highly charged election year against a much-hated president. It's certainly not too early now to consider what made 2006 different.

Almost without exception, the commentators analyzing the 2006 election downplayed the progressive parts, characterizing the large new crop of Democrats as overwhelmingly leaning right. "These Democrats that were elected last night are conservative Democrats," declared CBS News chief Washington correspondent Bob Schieffer. Now former editor of *The New Republic*, Beinart was back: "Now that they have taken the House (and probably the Senate), Democrats should start acting like Republicans."[1] On CNN, Andrea Koppel anticipated that the "new batch of moderate and conservative Democrats just elected . . . will force their party to shift towards the center." The next morning's *Washington Post* focused on the so-called Blue Dog Democrats (the ones coming from heavily Republican districts who often vote with the GOP). "Top Democrats such as Rep. Rahm Emanuel (Ill.) see these middle-of-the-road lawmakers as the future of the party in a nation that leans slightly right of center," reported the *Post*.

If the Blue Dogs drive the Congress's direction, they won't do it without help from conservative party players like Emanuel at the party's top. Forty-four Blue Dogs will contend for power with 63 left-leaning progressives and about 125 moderates. In the 2007 Congress, the Congressional Progressive Caucus will be the largest caucus in the House. The Democrats' majority in the Senate rests on as many dissidents from the left as from the right. In addition to the Senate's first self-described democratic socialist (Bernie Sanders in Vermont), the majority rests on winners, like Sherrod Brown in Ohio and Jon Tester in Montana, who broke with the Emanuel/Clinton Democrats on trade (Brown is the author of *Myths of Free Trade: Why American Trade Policy Has Failed*) and the USA Patriot Act. Challenged by Republicans in a debate, Tester shot back: "I don't want to weaken the Patriot Act, I want to repeal it." As for the notion that the nation "leans slightly right of center," polling showed that raising the minimum wage, extending health insurance to the uninsured, and changing course in Iraq were all majority positions in November 2006, as were keeping abortion legal and granting legal recognition to gay and lesbian relationships.

When it comes to analyzing elections, the training of public attention upward leaves a whole lot of the public out of the political picture. In a paean to a hometown boy, the *Chicago Tribune* declared that the incoming Congress was "The House that Rahm Built." Take that, you 3.5 million people on MoveOn's e-mail list, you thousands of small contributors, hundreds of DNC staffers, grassroots activists, unions, volunteer vote-protectors, and even a good number of the Democrats' own winning candidates: according to analysis like this, you don't count. "Now that the votes have been counted, the story of how Emanuel helped end an era of

Republican rule can be told, He did it, in large measure, by remaking the Democratic Party in his own image," wrote the *Tribune*. In fact, for many of the Democrats' breakthrough wins, Rahm Emanuel (who served as finance director for Bill Clinton's first campaign) can't claim credit. Anti-war David Loebsack, of Iowa, and New Hampshire's Carol Shea-Porter would never have entered the race if they had waited for an approving nod—or money—from the Democratic Congressional Campaign Committee (DCCC) or Emanuel. The Democrats' class of twenty-seven newcomers includes at least half a dozen supposedly long-shot candidates like Shea-Porter (who was once ejected from a Bush rally for wearing a "Turn Your Back on Bush" T-shirt), whose support came from the bottom—from local grass roots and virtual netroots—not the top.

It's time for a definition of terms. This book advises party Democrats to develop, not ditch, their base, by which I mean those demographic groups that vote disproportionately blue (the Democrats' color on those TV maps on election night). That includes members of trade unions, African Americans, Native Americans, Latinos, young voters (in 2006, a startling 70 percent of Hispanic voters voted Democratic), unmarried women (66 percent voted blue in 2006), religious minorities, and city dwellers. "Democrat" is a self-diagnosed state of being. Some Democratic voters love the label, even as its meaning remains up for grabs. My definition of a liberal is someone who longs for an imagined "good society" when things were kindlier, gentler, and fairer. My definition of a progressive is someone who believes the good old days weren't so great for many of us but the glory days might yet lie ahead, if we continue the kind of advance that forced the nation to pass civil rights laws, the Clean Air and Water acts, and almost (but not quite) the Equal Rights Amendment. Those on the Left, to a greater or lesser degree, hold to a belief that this whole society is set up to serve those with power and wealth, and oppress all those without. The leftists in this book are the ones who talk down electoral politics but increasingly engage in it anyway. They're in the Samuel Beckett school of politics ("I can't go on, I'll go on"). I've always been a big fan of Samuel Beckett.

The problems with see-no-people politics aren't only political, they're also pragmatic. Under the leadership of the centrist wing of the Democratic Party (those aligned with the neoliberal Democratic Leadership Council and Bill Clinton), the party bottled up money and power and decision-making in Washington, and chased big donations and centrist voters, leaving the majority of state party organizations to stumble along or rot. What they built is a Penthouse Party: all top-floor suites, no load-bearing walls, no foundations, no functioning stairway to the street. In 2004, in many states, the party lacked the means to perform basic functions. To register and turn out Democratic voters, the party relied on foot-soldiers-for-hire, people like Air America's listeners and hundreds of thousands of others who did the hard-slog work of engaging potential voters, talking to them face-to-face about issues they cared about, and persuading them to cast a ballot. Every likely foot soldier (and some very unlikely ones) turned out to do his or her bit to get Bush and Cheney out of office. But it wasn't enough.

Blue Grit is cram-packed with stories of those for whom foot-soldiering is not enough. Blue Grit democrats have been doing more than voting, they've been building institutions that do what a generation of politicians has not. They listen to what's going on, not in the suites but in the streets; they organize; and they stick around after the ballots are cast. Gloria Totten didn't like the candidates the old process was producing, so she started a program called Progressive Majority to recruit and train a farm team of candidates for office. "Progressives have organized, litigated, mobilized; we haven't engaged in the electoral arena. Now we are," Totten told me in the summer of 2006. Now the group is active in eight states, training candidates who are running for office up and down the ticket—from school board on up. "In 2006, we elected 76 new progressives to office in eight states . . . bringing the total number of progressives that Progressive Majority helped elect to 186 in just three short years," Totten reported on November 8, 2006.

The powerhouse youth group the League of Independent Voters (formerly the League of Pissed-Off Voters) wrote and distributed more than one hundred voter guides in 2004. In 2006 their online voter guide tool enabled activists to produce ninety local progressive guides that were used in thirty-eight states. The League was in Ohio in 2004, when voters were turned away by long lines caused by a shortage of voting machines in inner-city precincts. In 2006 the Ohio League knocked on more than 50,000 doors and turned out thousands of voters to the polls. When they saw poll workers pushing provisional ballots on new voters in eleven youth-heavy Columbus precincts, they sounded the alarm. Working with a coalition of volunteer election-protection groups that didn't exist in 2004, they forced the Board of Elections to educate precinct workers about Ohio voting laws—"which they did by late morning," and regular voting resumed, the League's national field director reported.

"It's a revolution," chirped a retiree who called in to *RadioNation* from Broward County, Florida, when she heard some Blue Grit democrats speak before the midterms of 2006. Elevated by age and electoral excitement and what sounded like relief, it was the highest-pitched "it's a revolution" I'd ever heard. I don't know that I totally agree, but I do know that as the country looks toward 2008, people without portfolio (and many of them without pay packet) are stepping in, and they're making a darn good stab at filling the vacuum, where a functioning, people-focused Democratic Party is not. Fed up with the party's priorities, people who for years sat disgusted on the sidelines are stepping up and doing more than vote. Tired of watching the way the party treats the very Americans upon which it depends for votes, people who once contented themselves with voting "least worst" are taking politics back.

I spent a year on the road, traveling the United States, checking, and it turns out not to be a talk-show host's late-night fantasy. It's true. Progressive change in America is not half as impossible or improbable as some people would like us to think. One question for blues with grit, it seems to me, is can they talk to their neighbors? Nobody has been talking to some folks for two decades—nobody but the organized Right. The question for Penthouse Democrats, on the other hand, is do they want to be the Blue Grit party? Rank-and-file people are taking politics back from their politicians for a reason: their lives and their communities demand relief. If the Penthouse Democrats don't respond, those same people just might take their skills and savvy someplace else.

New York City
November 14, 2006

CHAPTER ONE ☆ Where's the Party?

It goes on one at a time,

it starts when you care

to act, it starts when you do

it again and they said no,

it starts when you say We

and you know who you mean, and each

day you mean one more.

—MARGE PIERCY, "The Low Road,"
posted on the office wall of the
Progressive Leadership Alliance of Nevada[1]

I went looking for the Democratic Party. That was my first mistake. I assumed there was such a thing. I imagined that it hung out somewhere in a big office with a map of the country on the wall and a cash box at the door for lobbyists. Was it the Democratic National Committee? Howard Dean, chair of the DNC, told me it was not. State party chairs? I didn't find one who felt the state parties had much control over anything. Was it the presidential candidates? The party's hook-up with its presidential candidates is more like a fling than a meaningful relationship. Having been sold to the nation and the world as the party's most dearly beloved and best, when their campaigns lose, all but a handful of presidential contenders slither back down the leadership ladder to campaign another day (or more likely, to be begged not to). I did speak to several campaign managers of different sorts. Their answer to my question was some version of "Are we the Democratic Party? Heck no." In Congress, representatives of each of the big caucuses (the conservative Blue Dogs, the centrist Democratic Alliance, and the Congressional Progressive Caucus) will tell you that they are the party's true heart. No one has a better claim to be the party than the people who vote Democratic, but if *RadioNation* callers are an indication, even they spend a good part of every day railing at other Democrats. So, Democrats—where's the party?

I decided to start looking in the home state of the party's most powerful player in the U.S. Senate, Harry Reid. Nevada is a place in flux, a tantalizing prize for Democrats. Blue in the cities, red in the rural parts, Nevada's like the country at large in that plenty of Democrats live here, but they bunch up. There are Democratic clusters up north in Washoe County, mostly in the city of Reno and around the state capital, Carson City. Eighteen percent of the state population live in Washoe. Almost 70 percent of Nevadans cram into a single county, Clark, in the southernmost tip of the state. Home of Las Vegas and its surrounding townships, Clark's the only Nevada county that votes majority Democratic. But Nevada's numbers are increasing so fast that the census is struggling to keep up. It's the fastest-growing state in the nation. Every election there is a virtually new electorate. The state's population doubled in the 1980s and doubled *again* in the 1990s (up 66 percent compared with a national growth rate of 13 percent). Most of the newcomers gravitate to the cities. What people like to say about the rural counties, or "rurals," is that you need a helicopter for a day to find fifty voters, let alone fifty votes, and you'd need several days with a chopper if you were looking for that many Democrats.

Eighty-seven percent of Nevada is made up of federal lands, managed mostly by the Bureau of Land Management. Drive an hour into the canyons, and you'll find half a dozen people living per square mile, in isolation. Turn around and drive back toward Las Vegas, and the panorama is dense with neon lights, airport smog, and churning urban sprawl. Developers are digging new streets out of the desert faster than any map company can print up street maps, and the intersections are cluttered with drivers seeking a street that isn't where it was yesterday, or will be tomorrow.

It's a slippery state to get a handle on. It's equally hard to get a complete picture of Nevada Democrats. Senator Reid maintains three offices here (in Las Vegas, Reno, and Carson City), but like most U.S. senators, he's less likely to be in any one of them than he is to be back east in D.C. Reid's an idiosyncratic Democrat: Mormon, antichoice (he received a rating of 20 out of a 100 from NARAL Pro-Choice America in 2004), and careful what he says about gun control (Nevadans love their guns). In 2005 he scored points among progressives by forcing a closed session of the Senate to discuss the Bush administration's handling of intelligence in the run-up to the war in Iraq. But he's regularly under attack from the Left for his close relationships with lobbyists from corporations, trade groups, and most especially, his home-state tourism and gambling industry (or as they call it here, delicately, "gaming"). When he rose to minority leader in January 2005, six of Reid's former staffers were working as lobbyists on Capitol Hill. Soon after he was sworn in, "It was like a scene out of *The Godfather,*" one lobbyist told *Roll Call.* "He was in the back room and people were lined up to greet him and pay homage."[2] Facing no serious election threat, he has certainly used his incumbency to build a powerful war chest. According to the nonpartisan tracking group Political MoneyLine, Senator Reid's personal political action committee (or PAC) raised $2.2 million in 2005–2006. The Center for Responsive Politics reports that by the end of the season, Reid's PAC had spent $1,684,085 on Democratic candidates. Critics complain that all that money trading hands among politicians builds alliances among those in power that compete with those officials' ties to their own voters. Voters end up competing for attention not only with corporate lobbyists but also party elites. The progressive Las Vegas blogger Hugh Jackson calls Reid and his protégés "the Mormon Mafia." What also irritates Jackson and other local progressives is what they call the "non-aggression pact" Reid seems to have signed with Nevada's other senator, Republican John Ensign.

Nevada sends two Republicans and one Democrat to Congress. Governor Jim Gibbons is GOP. In Carson City, Democrats control the Assembly, Republicans the Senate. Reid is one face of the Democratic Party in Nevada. Looking for a different one, I found union shop steward Maggie Carlton. Carlton's "other" job is as a state senator in Carson City. (Nevada's civilian legislature meets once every two years for ninety days.) The rest of the time, Carlton works days as a waitress at the coffee shop in the Treasure Island casino. In Reno I found Assistant Majority Whip Sheila Leslie, a progressive state representative with a long history of working in nonprofits. Leslie's day job is specialty courts coordinator for the second judicial district court, where she runs the criminal family and juvenile drug courts and the state's first mental health court. In 2004, as John Kerry went down to defeat in her state, Leslie, whose campaign headquarters was her family's kitchen table, saw her share of the vote in a mixed district shoot up from 53 percent to 63 percent. Apparently voters liked her record as chair of the assembly's Health and Human Services Committee and as chair of the Joint Budget Subcommittee on Human Resources. She makes no bones about her politics. When asked to complete candidates' questionnaires, Leslie writes, "I have not served in the military, although I did serve as a Peace Corps Volunteer in the Dominican Republic (1979–1980)."

Like Maggie Carlton, Sheila Leslie is a nonpolitician who became fed up with politicians. "It's one thing to elect friends to office, but it's even better to elect members of the family," Carlton the union steward told me after work one night. "You don't have to go back and reeducate [politicians] who live it the same way you do." Says Sheila Leslie: "You can sit on the sidelines and whine about things, but I ran for office because no one else, no Democrat, would run in my district." Since coming to office in 1999, Leslie's succeeded in securing new funding for mental health and homelessness programs, including, in 2005, a $5 million appropriation for a new homeless shelter in Reno. She's worked with city cops to change the way the state treats addicts in the court system. Both women strongly supported then-governor Kenny Guinn's controversial budget in 2003, which included $1 billion in new taxes. If legislation like that can pass in a relatively conservative, largely libertarian state like Nevada, they believe it can pass anywhere, with good organizing. In 2007 both women will be returning to Carson City, Leslie for her fifth term, Carlton for her third. (Terms in assembly are shorter than those in the senate.)

If the party is its elected officials, in Nevada that group includes people like Leslie and Carlton. If the party is its voters, those include people like the volunteers at the Progressive Leadership Alliance of Nevada (PLAN), the most influential coalition of activist groups in the state, headed up by Leslie's ex-husband, Bob Fulkerson. Now in its thirteenth year, the PLAN alliance spans from labor to the gay equality movement. Among the forty member groups are the state chapters of the ACLU, the SEIU (the service workers' union), the AFL-CIO, and the Conservation League, as well as the Gay and Lesbian Community Center, the Reno-Sparks Indian Colony, the Nevada Immigration Coalition, and the Women's Lobby. It's a nonpartisan, nonprofit organization, but when potential candidates are thinking of running for office, it's PLAN that provides training workshops on the key issues. When voters are facing a mind-boggling array of initiatives on the ballot, it is PLAN that comes to the rescue, printing up handy voter guides that citizens can download from PLAN's website: "Confused about all the ballot questions? Take this to the polls with you." Since 2001 PLAN has been working with legislators to restore voting rights to former felons. Stage one of the legislation passed in 2003 with bipartisan support. (Next, PLAN would like the law to include more types of felons.) Liberal lobbyists meet every Wednesday in Leslie's office in the state capital. PLAN's members can bring no end of witnesses to testify in the legislature in support of the bills the legislators present. In 1999 the group built support for an LGBT nondiscrimination law and new workplace safety rules designed to protect non–English speakers. "Why do the blue-collar unions and the Catholic immigrants back the gay bills?" I asked Fulkerson, who answered simply, "Because they know the LGBT folks from PLAN meetings, and the LGBT groups backed the workplace safety act." In 2004 PLAN registered some seven thousand new voters, more than half of whom turned out to vote.

PLAN's partner in Clark County is Local 226 of the hotel and restaurant employees' union, UNITE/HERE. No entity does more than Local 226, the Culinary Workers Union, to mobilize Democratic voters in Clark. Nationally, the labor movement pulled out all the stops to elect Kerry/Edwards. The Service Employees International Union (SEIU) spent some $65 million in 2004. The AFL-CIO kicked in $45 million and mobilized five thousand workers paid full-time, and more than a quarter of a million volunteers to try to unelect George W. Bush. At the season's peak, one tenth of the members of the powerhouse Culinary Workers Union, or "the Culinary," as it's known in Las Vegas, was working in the streets to swell the vote. Most Culinary members were contributing a dollar a month to the union's election fund and yet more became involved in a nonpartisan campaign to raise the state minimum wage $1 above the federal rate of $5.15.

In the years since 2004, party-friendly commentators have released a mountain of analysis geared to winning Democrats back the White House. Some believe what the party needs is a grand welding together of all its various strands. Right now, the strange entity that gets called the big tent of the Democratic Party extends from big business, voting for the Democratic Leadership Council, to radical socialists stumping for members of the Congressional Progressive Caucus. Some suburban representatives are elected based on TV ads alone, with no party organization whatsoever; city representatives (like Maggie Carlton or Sheila Leslie) can come into office drawing solely on their community's or the union's support. Kerry and Edwards's defeat was enough to persuade some that the party needed unity. Specifically, they argued, interest groups (meaning prochoice advocates, environmentalists, and organized labor) needed to get in line and work more closely with the Democratic Party, rather than, as they have done, hold back their support and endorsements in exchange for party pledges on their issues.

"The way interest group politics are done in today's Democratic Party just has to change," wrote Michael Tomasky (then at the *American Prospect*) early in 2006. "We have to pull together, make some sacrifices and just sometimes look beyond our own interests to solve our problems."[3] Bloggers Markos Moulitsas and Jerome Armstrong put it even more strongly in their book, *Crashing the Gates.* "There is too much emphasis on what the party can do for them and not enough on what they can do for the party," wrote Kos (as he's known on his blog, Daily Kos) and Armstrong. "We could forgive the issue groups their dogged uncompromising fealty to their cause if it proved successful," they wrote, "but that hasn't been the case, at least not lately.... Today, labor appears more of an anachronism than a vibrant component of the modern progressive movement."

Labor doesn't look like an anachronism in Las Vegas in the hiring hall of the Culinary. Local 226 occupies a colorful, low, red-white-and-blue building with murals in the shadow of the madcap Stratosphere Las Vegas Hotel and Casino at one end of the legendary casino Strip. The sixty-thousand-member local is the fastest-growing private sector local in the country. Its accomplishments are legendary. In a right-to-work state (where workers may enjoy the benefits of union contracts without paying union dues), the Culinary has managed to organize every major casino and hotel on the strip. Nationwide, union members make up 12.5 percent of the population. In Clark County's hotel and casino industries, union density is topping 90 percent. When the union struck the Frontier Casino in 1991, not one of the Frontier's 550 unionized workers crossed the picket line for six and a half years. Wages in Las Vegas's casinos stand at 40 percent higher than those in nonunionized Reno. In a low-employment state with a flood of workers coming across the border from the south, it's in the Culinary's interest to help newcomers apply for citizenship—and union membership. Organizing the undocumented is not easy, but it's the way forward, D. Taylor, secretary treasurer of Local 226 told me: "Detroit's not coming back and it's government policy to let it go." The service sector is the fastest-growing part of the U.S. economy. "It's not as if there's a different workforce to organize; there's this one," said Taylor. Membership has tripled in the last ten years.

On the day I dropped by its offices, a wry, white-haired receptionist-cum-traffic-controller was juggling insurance claims, grievance procedures, press inquiries, and the latest leafleting mission. Just in case I was thinking that this particular morning was especially hectic, my neighbor in the waiting area put me straight. "You should have seen the action 'round here on Election Day."

Casino worker Santos Farias is a Culinary member. In 2004 he took a pay cut and a leave of absence from his job to knock on doors because he felt the election was important. "When Gore lost, I was so mad," Farias, who is originally from Nicaragua, told me. "I knew he won, and it was stolen from him. I hoped this time it would be different." Farias has a son in the service. He says he would have joined the military himself after September 11 and willingly fought in Afghanistan if he'd not been too old, but he opposed the war in Iraq: "We're in a war for nothing, and we have to stop it." Farias canvassed all summer long in the blazing Nevada sun. Sometimes it was 120 degrees and his shoes were melting on the tarmac. "Our members were out when the students from the Sierra Club couldn't hack it," declared Pilar Weiss, political director at the Culinary.

Critics would be better positioned to criticize the interest groups and call them to work more closely with the party if there was anything resembling a vibrant party in most states. Thanks to Harry Reid, the Nevada state party is actually in comparatively good shape, but I couldn't help wincing about how recent that state of affairs is. In early 2006 when I met Alison Schwartz—who directed the party's field campaign in 2004—she was excited. A Democratic candidate could win this place. "Absolutely, it's possible," she told me emphatically. "It's just going to take some work." On the day I showed up, the party's executive director was on maternity leave. Schwartz was on duty at the Democratic Party headquarters, in a low suburban shopping plaza in a township just outside Las Vegas. The party office could easily be mistaken for a shop. Storefront windows face out onto the street, stacks of papers pile up left and right. It looks like a place that's selling something, which of course it is. Schwartz sums the product up as "Democratic values," a phrase I heard from Democratic Party officials everywhere I went. What it means is harder to pin down. Schwartz tells me her area of expertise is organizing. She's thrilled about what she calls the new

Democratic Party machine in this state. Why "new" I ask with some trepidation. As Schwartz puts it, it's new because "before 2004, things were pretty skeletal." A political consultant who preferred to remain anonymous puts it more bluntly: "Before Reid took over leadership, there was no party in this state."

In 2004 the Nevada State Democratic Party spent almost $10 million building up what had been until that moment a pretty moribund operation. When Schwartz came here from Missouri in 2003, when she was in her twenties, the party had just installed a new computerized voter file. It's great, she tells me. Schwartz's volunteers could come back from door-knocking with new information and download their data from handheld computers directly onto the party file stored on the Web. No wonder she's excited. What did they have before the new online file, I queried. "With so many new people coming in and residents moving about, we just weren't able to keep up. We just had very dirty files." Former volunteers described it to me this way: after a day in Nevada's hot streets, they'd do their best to update the party's huge printed-out lists by hand, but the volunteers were unreliable. There was really no way for team leaders to keep track, and in between elections there were no team leaders; there was barely anyone on staff. When staff arrived, as Schwartz did, a year ahead of the vote (from out of state), they were virtually starting over. Old voter lists are not like wine. Sitting around and aging between elections, old lists of voters and volunteer information are about as useful as losing lottery tickets, especially in a high-turnover state like this one.

The party hired its first full-time communications director in 2003. When I heard that, my mind turned to Karen Hughes, who had directed the Republican Party in the run-up to George Bush's election as governor of Texas. It was in their years out of power that Texas Republicans turned what had been a blue state red. Bush's victory was the end, not the start, of that process. By full-time communications direc-tor, do you mean someone who works during the legislative session? I almost hated to ask. "You got it. We never had that before," Schwartz replied. "We beefed up a lot."

State parties are supposed to provide the constant presence that candidates' campaigns cannot. A year after the election, Ann Sheridan, Nevada state director of Kerry-Edwards 2004 Inc., was loath to criticize the candidate, the DNC, and least of all her colleagues, but looking back on the race still hurt. She couldn't talk about it face-to-face. "It was excruciating," she said via telephone. "Could things have been done differently?" I asked gently. It was like picking at a scab. Reticent, Sheridan admitted that there were some flaws in the process. There are always tussles over resources between the campaign staff at the na-tional level and in the states. The Nevada state campaign was well co-ordinated among statewide players, but there were some rough patches with Washington, she conceded. For one thing, by the time Sheridan's appointment was announced in early June, the Kerry campaign was al-ready under attack for failing to reach Latinos. The Bush/Cheney op-eration had offices up and running in heavily Latino swing states like Nevada, Arizona, and Florida all year. The word in the Latino commu-nity was that Kerry just didn't get it, said Sheridan. The lack of Latinos (and for that matter, African Americans and Asians) in Kerry's inner circle didn't go unnoticed in Nevada, where the Hispanic population is approaching 20 percent. In an effort to correct things, Kerry/Edwards brought New Mexico's governor Bill Richardson and former Housing and Urban Development secretary Henry Cisneros to Nevada. The Bush campaign had Spanish-speaking ads on Nevada radio all summer. Kerry's came in too few, too late. Part of the problem was waiting on federal matching funds. National money didn't kick in until after the nomina-tion was secured at the Democrats' National Convention in August.

The ads that did run in the interim were made by the New Democrat Network, a project of the Media Fund, a so-called 527 (named for its place in the tax code), which was banned from consulting with the campaign or the party and was barred from mentioning the name of the candidate. Sheridan, who knew the Kerry team from campaigns in Massachusetts, had little input in deciding how the campaign money was spent or on the campaign's messages, which she says were worked out by the pollsters and "the message professionals." The most telling example is the day that the man on the Nevada desk in D.C. wanted her in-state team to go through a dry run for Election Day a few weeks before November 2. "Don't get me wrong. Great idea. You learn a lot. Worth doing," Sheridan told me emphatically. "But it involved a huge investment of staff time and it took people away from what they were already doing, which, in the case of Nevada, was helping people who were voting." Nevada has two weeks of early voting in October. "They did it when we were in the middle of early voting. We said, Okay, if you really want to, but I was just incredulous. . . . You're pulling my team off the streets for your little fuckin' checklist exercise?"

After a hard-fought campaign, George W. Bush beat John F. Kerry in Nevada by three percentage points. Sheridan had to close up shop that very day. "Campaigns budget through Election Day, and that's it. It's foolish, not to mention agonizing," she said. "People are demolished, and you have to close up shop." Candidates say a variation of what John Edwards said in his concession speech: "You can be disappointed, but you cannot walk away. This fight has just begun. Together we will carry on and we will be with you every step of the way." And then, poof, "the whole thing just stops, comes to a huge and screeching halt, and in twenty-four hours everybody gets blown to the winds," says Sheridan with a wince. It's one heck of a way to build a movement.

In my search for the Democratic Party in Nevada, I found that even in a battleground state, the home of a party leader, most of the key campaign staff and the staffers at the state party were flown in from somewhere else. Why? Because for twenty years, the party has chosen to funnel money and control to Washington, letting the state parties shrivel and shrink. The practice of keeping leaders powerful and the infrastructure poor reached its zenith under the leadership of Bill Clinton and the Democratic Leadership Council, a probusiness group. The years of economic growth during the 1990s were a good time to draw in dollars from corporate interests and lobbyists. Signing the North American Free Trade Agreement, or NAFTA, Clinton chose business's side over labor's. Labor strongly opposed the deal, but corporate lobbyists were all for it. The cost of alienating grassroots labor voters was hard to measure—the biggest labor federation, the AFL-CIO, still produced its endorsements and worked for Democratic candidates. Contributions from business to the DNC, meanwhile, piled up. By the time Clinton's ally Terry McAuliffe left the DNC in 2004, the organization had brand-new headquarters in Washington, a shiny example of all that the state parties did not have. McAuliffe's fund-raising skill and Bill Clinton's charismatic leadership put a great facade on the national party, but across the states its infrastructure was pretty much hollowed out. When the Democrats lost in 2002 what had been their beachhead—power in Congress—the corrosion within revealed itself. Now that they had no more Lincoln bedroom, no more swanky receptions in the Capitol Rotunda, no more control over any branch of government, the ardor of the K Street lobbyists cooled. Worse, the day after that election the McCain/Feingold Bipartisan Campaign Reform Act (BCRA) took effect. BCRA banned soft-money contributions to the national party. Democrats were in trouble: they had to reach millions of new voters, but they were sorely lacking ground troops.

Democratic leaders got it. They had to do something they hadn't done in a while—namely, organize on a massive scale—and they had to do it in a new way. They could have diversified the funding base, chased more small donations, and pumped money into the states. But they didn't do that. Instead, former top Clinton aide Harold Ickes, the AFL-CIO's Steve Rosenthal, and Ellen Malcolm of the prochoice PAC known as Emily's List came up with a way to create a parallel party called a 527. It looked like the Democratic Party—and it was headed by party people—but under tax law it was a separate entity, permitted to take a partisan approach to issues but not to promote any specific candidate.

The challenge of looking for the Democratic Party in Nevada was exacerbated after 2004 by the fact that for all the action in this state, many of the actors weren't Democrats, at least not officially. They weren't even Nevadans. Nevada was one of seventeen states targeted by the DNC for a concerted campaign and just about every election-related nonprofit or 527 group sent in its folks. The largest liberal 527, America Coming Together, or ACT, placed some twenty full-time workers in the state. A short flight from California brought eager-beaver campaigners in on the same airplanes and coaches that carry other gamblers to the Silver State, and they came with the same great dream in their hearts of beating the odds and scoring the win that would finally, this time, make all the difference.

Jane McAlevey, executive director of SEIU local 1107 in Las Vegas, considers 2004 the high-water (or bottom-of-the-barrel) mark for the last-minute foot-soldier approach. In an essay written shortly after the election, McAlevey commented that the union motto "Don't mourn—organize!" had been corrupted into "Don't mourn—mobilize!" There's a difference. "In the 2004 presidential election, we set the movement record for mobilizing. And we lost," she wrote. ACT put 1,400 can-vassers in Las Vegas on Election Day and still there weren't enough Democrats statewide to pull off a victory. Democrats and their most prominent liberal allies had gotten very good at canvassing, polling, and turning out supporters—very good at mowing the grass roots. But sowing new grass? That calls for giving people new ways to think about their circumstances and new ways to consider their own power. To grow a constituency you have to work with people not once every four years, but year in, year out, and take them, politically speaking, from where they start out to the point where they are receptive to progressive arguments. "There are simply no shortcuts," wrote McAlevey. "We know because we have spent the past twenty years looking for one and have not found it."[4]

In 2004, 527 groups were the shortcut. The ban on coordination among the 527s and the party and campaign operations led to a lot of overlapping efforts. In the last few weeks of the campaign, Pilar Weiss of the Culinary Workers received a call from a union member who was working the streets. By that point every door in Clark and Washoe counties had been knocked on a dozen times, sometimes in one weekend. Weiss's caller was standing on a street corner about to approach a house on his list. He had a question: "Pilar, what shall I do? There's a line of five other canvassers from five other groups lined up right behind me."

On the day after the election, the vast majority of ACT volunteers got back on their planes and buses (and yes, even bikes), and returned to where they had come from. Phones were disconnected, voter-contact lists taken away. On *RadioNation* I heard a lot of heartbreak. The disappointment of losing is one thing, but what really got to callers was the sense that the day after the election they were on their own again, left with nothing and no one to connect to. "Tony from Marin" described his experience in an e-mail. "I traveled to Nevada at my own expense with a dozen friends to *do* something. In the eighteen months since that time all the energy and air was let out of the balloon of activism, and I'm finding that somehow now I'm on nobody's active list."

It wasn't that way on the Republican side. There, the Republican National Committee had pored over research that showed that in 2000, union households turned out to vote at higher rates than their percentage in the population, while evangelicals were underperforming, especially in the final hours of the race, when union mobilizations had their strongest effect. The RNC's response was to develop its 72-Hour Plan. Premiering in 2002, and reappearing in 2004 and 2006, it drew on the power of grassroots membership groups like the National Rifle Association, prolife organizations, and the congregations of right-wing churches. The GOP's field operation relied on volunteers, not flown-in paid staff. In 2004 the GOP's strategy network claimed to have deployed 300,000 volunteers, mostly to work within its own social network. "It's love and belief in the importance of the president," Ken Mehlman, Bush's campaign manager, claimed in an interview with the *New York Times.* "You can't, in politics and in almost anything you do, force people to do anything. They have to want to do it."[5]

In 2008 Democratic Party officials plan to hold a new early presidential caucus in Nevada the week before the New Hampshire primary. The state's early insertion in the schedule is a nod to the growing and diverse population of the Southwest and to the advances Democrats have been making in western states. Seeing opportunity in the West to build strength to match the GOP's lock on the heartland and the South, Democrats will be coming to Nevada to show their commitment to a region they hope will help them win the White House. When they trek out to Las Vegas and then hop north to Reno, will Democratic hopefuls find a state where interest groups have fallen more obediently in line? I doubt it. If things continue to proceed as they have in Nevada, progressive Democrats and their interest-group allies will enter 2008 more confident, not less.

Harry Reid absorbed a lot of spotlight on election night, 2006. His party's gains under his leadership were great. His home state of Nevada, however, was not one where Democrats made much progress. Democrats won four statewide offices, including treasurer and secretary of state, proving Democrats are capable of winning statewide office, but former senate president Dinah Titus lost her bid to be governor; Tessa Hafen, a Reid protégée and former staff member, narrowly lost her congressional race; and Senate contender Jack Carter (Jimmy Carter's son) was defeated by incumbent Republican John Ensign. Blogger Hugh Jackson believes Reid could have campaigned more vigorously against John Ensign. "Reid could have made this a Senate battleground but he didn't," humphed Jackson just before Election Day.

On the local state level, the Culinary helped Democrats pick up a seat on the all-important Clark County Commission (which governs the Strip and, unlike the legislature, meets full-time, not once every two years for ninety days). Weiss had twenty employees working full-time on the election, 120 in the week before the vote. The Democratic win on the commission knocked out an antiunion rising GOP star. "They spent $1.2 million to our $200,000 but we showed them," chuckled Weiss on November 10. Democrats also added one member to the assembly, giving them a 27–15 edge, and they narrowed GOP control of the senate to 11–10. In 2007 the U.S. House won't be the only chamber making history with its first female speaker. Barbara Buckley, a prochoice, proenvironmentalist Democrat with a career in public service, will be the first female leader of the Nevada house. Assistant Majority Whip Sheila Leslie ran virtually unopposed. She was reelected with close to 76 percent of the vote.

"When we founded PLAN, the Democratic old guard told us we didn't need a progressive coalition. They said we had one—the Democratic Party. We thought differently," Fulkerson reflects. Rooted in communities, with relationships that have been built up over time, PLAN, like the Culinary and the Nevada AFL-CIO, has been able to advance progressive policy ideas that win, even in this relatively conservative state where massive mining and casino corporations used to rule the roost. They've turned out votes for Kerry and Edwards and before that Clinton and Gore, but they've also elected their own. Even before the vote in 2006, Fulkerson was grooming a PLAN member to run for Leslie's seat when she is term-limited out in 2008.

In 2006 Nevadans voted for the second time (as their state law requires) to amend their constitution to raise the minimum wage. As in 2004, the wage hike was the most popular thing on the ballot. Nevadans voted 2 to 1 to raise the wage; it passed in every county, in the cities and the rurals both. (Nevada was one of six states to pass increases in the minimum wage above the $5.15 federal rate in 2006. No wage measure was defeated.) Nevadans also passed a tough restriction on smoking and turned down a weaker proposal backed by the tobacco industry, and they succeeded in keeping a treasury-capping ballot measure modeled on Colorado's Tax Payer's Bill of Rights (TABOR) off the ballot. The incoming governor, Republican Jim Gibbons, is under pressure to maintain full funding for kindergarten and the appropriations for mental health and homelessness that were in his predecessor's budget.

Calling for party unity behind today's Democratic Party is sort of like calling an army to fall in line behind a Wizard of Oz behind the curtain. It's hard to build a political party when, as critics complain, its constituency groups are tugging it in a dozen different directions, but when they blame special-interest groups for throwing too many ideas into the mix, critics are denigrating the groups that are turning out Democratic votes and advancing the ideas that are growing the progressive movement, even in red states.

On the day after the 2006 election, Pilar Weiss and her colleagues were right back at the Culinary. "We doubled our efforts in 2004, but we didn't fundamentally change what we do," she said. "This union's big on keeping our members involved. We're not big on just handing out checks to politicians." Electing labor's friends, ousting working people's enemies, encouraging union members to run for office: it's ongoing work, concluded Weiss. (She might have added, it's organizing, not mobilizing.) "We were doing it before 2004 and we've been here since."

The biggest challenge facing the union movement in Nevada is the 2005 split between the AFL-CIO and a breakaway group including the Teamsters and the SEIU. Because unions can affiliate at the national as well as state level, the relationships in Nevada seem to be holding up (the two groups worked side-by-side to win the wage initiative), but it will be interesting to see how it will play out in 2008. At the Culinary, D. Taylor believes the dispute threw up legitimate questions about union priorities: "We are here to serve our members, not any politician," he told me when we broadcast *RadioNation* live from the Culinary's hiring hall. "Eight years in office and the Democrats never got us labor law reform. Instead we got NAFTA. Republicans reward their friends, Democrats seem to reward their enemies."

Danny Thompson, of the state AFL-CIO, believes labor is holding up its side of the bargain with Democrats. Union members continue to constitute a quarter of all Democratic voters, even as their presence in the workforce has decreased. The fact that so many Nevadans voted for the minimum-wage increase and also George W. Bush suggests it's the party that needs to do better associating itself with workers' issues, says Thompson. Kerry could have done better here, he believes, if he'd just aligned himself more with the minimum-wage initiative. Says Gail Tuzzolo, who worked with Thompson on the "Give Nevadans a Raise" campaign, "It was like pulling teeth just to get the candidate to mention it."

Democrats coming to Nevada in 2008 better prepare for some interesting campaigning. Asked if he thinks the party's ready to share power with movement groups like his, Fulkerson hesitates, then responds: "I think they're getting more comfortable. They'd better." You can't just parachute into states and cultivate a grassroots base, he believes. "It's a long-term project." Nominating caucuses are decided by turnout, so the best-organized groups will dominate. In addition, PLAN's planning on holding an early candidates' forum where PLAN members will be able to judge the candidates for themselves. "We'll bring people in from the barrios and off the reservations and make the candidates tell us where they stand on our issues, face-to-face," says Fulkerson. The Culinary's planning on doing much the same thing. State senator Maggie Carlton told me, "When the candidates come out here, service workers are going to be asking them some tough questions about where they stand on immigration, the minimum wage, Medicaid, and social security, and they're going to have to answer."

Croupiers in Vegas say you can't bet against the house and win, but D.C. Democrats better not be counting on the same maxim holding true in politics. A cohort of Nevada organizers has its sights set on taking over the house.

CHAPTER TWO ☆ Red-State Blues

"We will not stand for it anymore! No more lies!
No more preemptive illegal war based on false information!
No more 'God is on our side' religious nonsense
to justify this immoral illegal war!"

—ROSS "ROCKY" ANDERSON,
mayor of Salt Lake City, Utah
August 2006

I did not expect that it would be in Utah I would meet my first transgendered church minister. But it was. The Reverend Sean Parker Dennison, the bearded leader of the South Valley Unitarian Universalist Society, takes services every week in a modern pine-and-concrete building whose gables are as high-pitched as his preaching voice.

As I searched for progressive change in unexpected places, I was looking for surprises, but Reverend Dennison was more than surprising. His smile, his beard, and his voice screamed anywhere-but-Utah. On the Sunday before the Dr. King holiday, families filed through the front doors of the reverend's South Valley church, beneath a large "Hate Free Zone" rainbow flag hanging over the entrance. The service featured a reading of a short biography of Dr. King and a poem by Mary Oliver, a lesbian naturalist.

"We have a dream of a community where all are accepted," sermonized the round-faced reverend. The one hundred or so congregants nodded in agreement, their heads bobbing an assortment of ski caps, suburban blue rinses, and sandy-colored rasta-wannabe dreadlocks.

Utah is hardly the world's most tranny-welcoming spot. It's better known for its adoration of lackluster Republican presidents and Mormon edicts than for any fondness toward those whose gender expression is out of the ordinary. Salt Lake City, just down the road from the South Valley church, is home to the world headquarters of the Church of Jesus Christ of Latter Day Saints (known colloquially as the Mormon Church). The LDS Church has some fixed ideas about gender. Transgendered s/he people have no place in the church handbook, but homosexuals do: they're punishable by excommunication (yes, they still do that here), followed by everlasting damnation.

The color of Utah, on those election-night Electoral College maps, is not ambiguous. The state hasn't voted for a Democrat for president since 1964. In 2004 Utah gave George W. Bush his widest victory margin (72 to 26 percent), and a year after his second inauguration, when his approval ratings had plummeted into the thirties nationally, Utahans were still giving W his highest thumbs-up numbers. Heck, thirty years ago the majority of Utahans still approved of the way Richard Nixon did his job, even after Watergate, even after his resignation.

The Utah I had mentally pictured was a sober place dominated by the conservative LDS Church. That state was the last in the nation to recognize Dr. King's birthday (and when it did, the Utah legislature initially—and begrudgingly—called it Human Rights Day). And yet here I was, listening to a transgendered minister read Mary Oliver in honor of Dr. King, and heads were nodding. Clearly my idea of Utah was in need of an update.

It's not just me. The mental picture that progressives in general tend to have of this country is not just snobbish; it's wrong on the local details and self-defeating. Utah is a case in point. The state is red, but Salt Lake City is as blue as they come, led by a mayor, now in his second term, who greeted President Bush, when he came to town in August 2006, not with a motorcade and a lunch at the historic Salt Lake City Town Hall but with a five-thousand-strong antiwar, anti-Bush demonstration. Mayor Ross "Rocky" Anderson excoriated the administration to a cheering crowd for the second year in a row. In 2005, when the president came to Salt Lake to address the Veterans of Foreign Wars, the mayor, worried that the demonstrations might be too small, sent out an e-mail to egg local organizers on, to show the president the "biggest demonstration" the state had ever seen.

That election-night television map messes with our heads. It certainly doesn't take into account a place like Salt Lake City. Nor is Utah an anomaly. The red-blue sandwich of a country shown on the map features blue Democratic crusts encasing a fat, red Republican filling. The picture accompanies all that doom-and-gloom-laden talk about a great cultural divide, but the United States more closely resembles a purplish smorgasbord than a red-blue sandwich. The country is dotted with blue. Every single American city with a population of over half a million voted for John Kerry in 2004, and half of all cities with over fifty thousand inhabitants did the same. Just as significant as the differences between the states are the political divisions within them. "Within this purple haze of our politics, a deep blue urban archipelago of voting does stand out," wrote University of Wisconsin professor Joel Rogers in *The Nation* not long ago. "Stretching across the country, it marks the islands of city life."

Cities lean left. It's no surprise why. Magnets for the risk-inclined, the boredom-averse, the desperate, the aspiring, and those who don't fit in someplace else, cities concentrate exactly those populations—blue collar, minority, poor, queer, and renting—that are most hurt by the politics of feed the rich, scapegoat the weak, and shift the wealth up from the bottom. In a period in which federal budgets have prioritized wars and tax cuts for the already-affluent over public needs and urban development grants (especially grants to Democrat-run cities), cities have felt the impact first. And they've fought back. More than 120 communities have passed living-wage initiatives, raising wages as high as $12 an hour for firms that contract with municipal governments. In the run-up to the invasion of Iraq, 165 cities and towns, from Vermont to Alaska, and Atlanta to Chicago, passed resolutions opposing unilateral war. More than 350 communities signed resolutions refusing to cooperate with the USA Patriot Act. Chicago alderman Joe Moore, working with Karen Dolan and John Cavanagh at the Institute for Policy Studies, has been pulling together a Cities for Progress network that Cavanagh estimates could ultimately include some four hundred cities that share a record of opposing war, approving living-wage ordinances, reducing greenhouse gases (which cause global warming), and regulating predatory "big box" stores like Wal-Mart.

In 2005 University of Wisconsin professor and political strategist Joel Rogers and Madison mayor Dave Cieslewicz convened a meeting of New Cities mayors. From the original dozen, the attendance at New Cities meetings grew to forty-five in a year and a half, most of them mayors, many from cities with liberal-to-left reputations (such as Berkeley and Madison), but some from surprising places too, like Salt Lake City and Boise, Idaho. The phenomenon is gaining momentum. Rogers estimates that even when narrowly defined, cities account for about 25 percent of the total U.S. population; add their suburbs, and you get a national majority; add the suburbs connected to what Rogers calls the "metro core," and you've got upwards of 80 percent of the country and the majority of the nation's wealth. They're the natural pillars of "high road economics," Rogers believes. Brought together under the banner of what is being called the Apollo Alliance, New Cities mayors—like Anderson—share an interest in encouraging smart, environmentally sound development that creates good jobs for low-income residents and cuts costs. (In 2006 Los Angeles mayor Antonio Villaraigosa continued his commitment to lead a fight for energy independence and job creation by "greening" deteriorating city buildings.)

"In most nations, cities are a big deal," exclaims Rogers. "But in America cities are the neglected stepchildren, exploited and abused when not simply ignored. Often they are portrayed as rank collections of pathology, modern Gomorrahs, deserving of destruction, and often enough they get it." At the think tanks where Democratic Party priorities are set, cities and the people who lead them don't seem to count for much. The 2004 Democratic National Convention didn't put a single mayor onstage in prime time. John Kerry campaigned in northern California without once appearing with popular San Francisco mayor Gavin Newsom (presumably because he didn't want the taint of a man who had approved same-sex marriage). When immigrants flooded into the streets nationwide in the spring of 2006 and President Bush was posing as their Spanish-speaking friend, the Democratic Party could have lined up behind the very popular Antonio Villaraigosa, mayor of the country's second-largest city, Los Angeles. Villaraigosa, whose father was a Mexican immigrant, could have punctured Bush's posturing. But the blue-state bluebloods of the Democratic leadership didn't do that. The party establishment keeps city leaders at a distance.

At the level of national two-party politics, says John Cavanagh of the Institute for Policy Studies, "we've got four hundred cities and towns that represent some sixty to seventy million Americans who never add up to anything." The core of the conservative movement, meanwhile, is about 20 to 30 million people (members of the National

Rifle Association and various Christian Right organizations). "They add up to everything," he sighs.

Why do Democratic leaders dismiss city leaders whose success hints at possibilities for progressive change? Perhaps it's because in recent years, while conservative Republicans have taken control of every branch of the federal government and most state governments, cities have elected a new generation of progressives of exactly the sort that the conventional wisdom in Democratic Washington says are too far out for our culturally divided nation. Cities aren't states—that's true enough. Thanks to redistricting and the lack of proportional representation in state legislatures, even a rock star of a city leader finds it hard to rise to governor in a starchy rural state, let alone senator. But there are examples: Senator Dianne Feinstein was mayor of San Francisco; former Baltimore mayor Martin O'Malley was elected governor of Maryland in 2006; and former GOP mayor of Chattanooga Bob Corker won a senate seat in Tennessee. The bigger point is, if the party's interested in tackling—rather than simply succumbing to—that cultural divide, it would be worth listening to lefty mayors in red states because they're doing just that.

Look at Utah. In November 1999, by a 60–40 majority, Salt Lake City voters elected Ross "Rocky" Anderson, an ACLU board member, mayor of Utah's biggest city. In contrast to the tread-quietly-and-try-not-to-disturb-the-horses style advised by Democratic bigwigs, Rocky's style tends more toward the bull-in-a-china-shop. He's the kind of guy who once made headlines for chasing a speeding limo driver down the interstate "because he felt other motorists were in danger." When I mention that the gay rodeo is in town, Rocky (as he is called by everyone) tells me that he's ridden in it. When his e-mail to antiwar activists urging them to demonstrate against Bush went public, Rocky didn't back down. He went and spoke to the VFW before the president and defended his right to protest Bush's policies. "What's hurting Salt Lake

City security? George Bush's state funding cuts are hurting the city's security," Anderson told *RadioNation*.

A lot of people would say that Anderson is successful in Salt Lake City because the city is the one part of Utah where the conservative religious majority is in the minority. According to polling, just under half of the city's residents say they're members of the LDS Church; politically, those who identify as Democratic, Republican, and independent claim roughly a third of the population each. But it's not as if Anderson avoids tough issues. In 1999 Anderson campaigned for office on a pledge to fire the city's chief of police, to stop what he called a "sprawl mall" by the airport, and to expand the city's light-rail public-transit system, all of which he did, despite opposition. In 2002 he hosted a successful Winter Olympics despite post-911 fears that the games would be a flop. During his tenure as mayor he's tangled with both the LDS Church establishment and his colleagues at the ACLU over city planning and other issues, but he has emerged more or less unscathed. In 2003 he was reelected with another healthy majority, whereupon he dedicated himself to changing the city's energy habits. The federal government was foot-dragging on global warming—Anderson made the city comply with the Kyoto Protocols for reducing greenhouse gases. He was the only U.S. mayor invited to speak at a global-warming conference in Argentina, where he discussed how his city met Kyoto's 2012 deadlines years in advance. Every traffic light in town has been converted to energy-saving luminescent diodes, as has every bulb in City Hall—even the Christmas tree lights. The imposing portraits of the city's former leaders now bask in a slightly cooler light than they once did, but even among his critics, feelings toward Anderson have warmed.

Restaurant owner Mark Hale is just one example of an Anderson convert. A devout member of the LDS Church who doesn't hesitate to explain in detail certain aspects of his beliefs, Hale hardly fits the stereotype of a man likely to embrace a progay, progreen, lapsed-LDS, ACLU activist like Anderson. In fact, when an extension of the light-rail system was proposed to run right down the middle of the street on which he has the star restaurant in his pizza-parlor chain, Hale had such fears about how the construction would disrupt his business that he convened a Committee to Stop East-West Light Rail to fight it. When Anderson first came to office, the Utah Transit Authority and Hale's business coalition were at loggerheads and the project was at a stand-still. The weekend after his inauguration, Anderson invited residents from the neighborhoods that would be affected by light-rail construction to his home and served them dinner and offered them a chance to talk. He helped negotiate a deal that included free advertising by the city for the businesses affected by the construction, and a bonus for the contractors if they treated the businesses well. The mayor also set up a twenty-four-hour complaint hotline, and was known to show up in the street himself at three A.M. to stop a jackhammer operator.

Hale couldn't be more impressed. "Now I talk about it as an example of government at its best," he says, and he's been invited to other states and communities to share his experience. He doesn't remember if he voted for Anderson the first time, but he did the second and he would again. "Rocky was very diplomatic, very insightful. He's a man of beliefs and he does what he believes. You've gotta love someone with that chutzpah," Hale told me. (There's another surprise: when they feel exuberant, Mormons, just like New Yorkers, suddenly speak Yiddish.)

In January 2006, 62 percent of Salt Lakers judged the mayor's job performance fair, good, or excellent—about double the percentage of Americans who felt that way about their president. Looking at similar numbers before the mayor's reelection, one Republican lobbyist concluded, "Lots of people, myself included, don't like a lot of Rocky's positions. But he wins respect for his forthrightness, passion, and hard work."[1]

. . .

One organization that Anderson has yet to win over is the Utah Democratic Party. In January 2006 the mayor delivered a stirring State of the City address to the city council. He touted the city's progress on just about every front and then talked about the challenges that remained. Among others, the mayor singled out homophobia, underscored by one suburban cinema owner's cancellation of *Brokeback Mountain* (familiarly known as the "gay cowboy movie"). The cancellation was "especially disturbing," Anderson said, in light of the same cinema's continued marketing and screening of *Hostel,* generally reviewed as one of the sickest and most disturbing films ever made. "Apparently, some members of our community find this despicable, sick, women-hating film more acceptable than a beautifully rendered love story," Mayor Anderson told the council, to applause from the public sitting in the audience.

The afternoon after Anderson's address, I visited the headquarters of the Utah Democratic Party. Jeff Bell, the Utah Democratic Party's communications director, was visibly irritated. "Did he have to take on the most powerful businessman in Salt Lake?" he muttered. A large, blustery, red-headed Utahan, Bell has been on the job—to invigorate the state party's message—for four months, thanks to a grant from the DNC. Bell believes Democrats in Utah need to talk more about their Christian religious beliefs. ("I am pretty singled in on Christian message because that's my eighty-nine percent majority here," he explains.) The Democrats, he reckons, need more Christianity and more effective sound bites: "My job is shaping the message of the state party chair to fit into sound-bite media," he says. But Rocky's words aren't Bell's kind of sound bites. "Much as I respect the guy, let's just say Rocky doesn't make my job any easier," Bell quips. He's keen to clarify that he's speaking in a personal, not an official, capacity, but it's not hard to pick up on the basic party line. The cartoons on the office wall poking fun at Anderson are not officially sanctioned, either, I'm sure, but they create a clear impression that the Democratic Party of Utah considers Anderson less a blessing than a curse.

The antagonism goes way back. In 1996 Anderson made a bid for a congressional seat that establishment Democrats were all geared up to claim without a primary for their own favorite candidate, Jim McConkie. McConkie, who had previously failed in a bid for the same congressional district, represented everything the conservative wing of the party was about. As one local politics reporter put it, McConkie "made his adherence to Mormon values the number one reason he should be nominated by the party and elected to office." McConkie conformed exactly to the recommendations of a (then) recent Brigham Young University poll that concluded that only a conservative white male Mormon Democrat stood a chance of winning statewide office in Utah. Anderson looked at Utah's second congressional district, which represents all of Salt Lake City and had been represented by successful liberal Democrats for years in the 1960s and 1970s, and thought differently. Saying he wouldn't have entered the race if "a person with a solid record of achievement and a commitment to a core of Democratic values" had entered, Anderson filed to run. The party's selection process, he felt, amounted to race, gender, and political profiling. McConkie pulled out in a huff and complained that the state party had been kidnapped by "special interests."

"Special interests" is the favorite term used by centrist and conservative Democrats to refer to what others consider the party's progressive base. Democratic Leadership Council founder Al From seems never to have seen a part of the Democratic base he didn't consider a "special interest." When the juggernaut of Ronald Reagan Republicanism rolled over Walter Mondale in 1984, winning every state but Minnesota and D.C., to Democrats, including Bill Clinton and Al From, the old New

Deal and civil-rights-era Democratic coalition was finished. Al From organized the DLC to "reform" the party by shoving "special interests" out of it, and soon thereafter Bill Clinton became a member. In a famous memo to prospective DLC members, From blamed the Democrats' decline on the "consistent pursuit of wrong-headed, losing strategies" of Mondale, which he described as "making blatant appeals to liberal and minority interest groups in the hopes of building a winning coalition, where a majority, under normal circumstances, simply does not exist."[2]

In Utah the DLC-Mondale debate played out in microcosm. The GOP's first clean sweep of Utah's congressional delegation happened in 1980, the year Reagan scooped up over two thirds (72.8 percent) of Utah's presidential vote against Jimmy Carter and a third-party candidate named John Anderson. Reagan's popularity cemented a two-to-one majority that Republicans have enjoyed in state government ever since. Anderson's entry into the 1996 second congressional district primary amounted to a showdown between the two wings of the Utah Democratic Party that had flapped at each other since 1980. The top of the party hierarchy believes in appealing to the dominant religion and preaching the gospel of Democratic Mormonism; the activist rank and file (many of whom are also Mormon) are concerned about overwhelming LDS influence and have a hard time telling the me-too Mormon Democrats and the GOP apart.

In the 1996 primary, after McConkie dropped out, Rocky's opponent turned out to be another establishment hand-pick: ten-year legislator Kelly Atkinson. In the view of his critics and his supporters both, Atkinson wore his LDS membership on his coat, his hat, *and* his sleeve. He ran against Rocky primarily on the grounds that the ACLU board member's support for choice and for equal rights for gays and lesbians, and his opposition to the death penalty, would make him unelectable. It didn't help Anderson that early in the campaign a reporter asked if he'd support the federal Defense of Marriage Act, and he said he wouldn't.

(It was "disgraceful election-year pandering," he thought, that wasn't worthy of the U.S. Congress.) Later, when asked more specifically if he supported same-sex marriage, he replied, "I believe everyone should have the equal protection of the law, regardless of race, gender or sexual orientation."[3] That, as Anderson told me, was that. "The media went nuts." But on Primary Day, Atkinson, not Anderson, was roundly routed. The vote came in 55 to 44 percent for Rocky.

What happened next depends on who you talk to. Conservatives at Democratic Party headquarters will say that Anderson went on to lose the general election, just as every consultant on the right predicted he would. His supporters say Anderson went on to run a very respectable race against Merrill Cook, a GOP explosives-manufacturer-turned-perennial-candidate-for-office whose campaign benefited from some swift-boat type of dirty tricks. There's no denying, a couple of weeks before Election Day, when one poll showed the candidates neck and neck, pink flyers showed up all over Salt Lake County claiming to come from "Utah Gay and Lesbian for Anderson Committee." The flyers described Anderson as "pro-abortion, pro gun control, pro ACLU, pro gay clubs in school." The committee, needless to say, did not exist. Rocky lost his run for Congress. His opponent got 129,963 votes; Anderson, 100,283.

"The second district belonged to us. . . . We gave it away," one member of the central committee of the Utah Democratic Party told the media. The party leadership's response to Anderson's insurrection was to try to kill the primary system. Anderson's response is "Who is 'us'?" He can run the numbers: 40 percent of the district self-identify as Republicans, 22 percent as Democrats, and 36 percent as Independents.[4] It's certainly not a liberal place, but liberals have represented it. Former three-term governor Cal Rampton (who campaigned for Anderson in 1999) ran the state for twelve years as a liberal Democrat (1965–1977), and as he pointed out on the campaign trail, "it fared rather well." The mayor still believes he could have won the race if he'd had a unified party behind him—or even some party money.

According to FEC filings, Republican Merrill Cook spent over a million dollars to Anderson's $400,000. "Imagine spending over $1 million to repeat how one stands for traditional family values, while your liberal opponent supports same-sex marriage?" Anderson asked me, still smarting. "From the Democratic Party I got zip. . . . They wouldn't even list my name on their election materials for fear I'd taint their other candidates." In the *Rocky* movies, Balboa, played by Sylvester Stallone, didn't have a corner man who was actively working against him. (If he had had one, there would never have been a *Rocky*, let alone *Rocky II* and *III*.)

Utah progressives, it may be said, are to American liberals what anti-Bush Americans are to foreign observers of the United States: a phenomenon for which there is little obvious evidence. But progressives in other parts of America have more in common with Utahans than they might imagine, and they may have more to learn from the place than they anticipate. As one activist here put it, in the last quarter century the rest of the country has become more like Utah, not the other way around. For example, Utah has long known one-party government: the GOP has dominated the state legislature for the past twenty-five years. Yet even in that chilly environment for progressives, Rocky Anderson has been winning victories, raising issues that need to be talked about. And he's not the only person in Utah doing that.

The discussion now going on in national Democratic circles has been gripping Utah for two decades. According to the conventional narrative, ever since Utahans fell in love with Ronald Reagan the GOP has been unstoppable. Chip Ward, Utah nature writer and activist, believes that, to the contrary, progressives have not put up a fight. Especially on the environmental front. Ward is confident that the potential for progress exists in places traditional progressives write off.

Religious conservatives aren't as monolithically opposed to environmentalism as progressives sometimes think. According to a survey by the Pew Forum on Religion and Public Life, solid majorities of all major American religious groups back stronger measures to protect the environment, and some conservative evangelicals have recently started speaking out about a biblical obligation to protect all of "creation." A tendency on the Democratic side to simply write off certain groups means that those groups are hearing from only one side.

Chip Ward says that if he'd listened to what people said was "possible" in Utah, he'd never have gotten anything done, but like Mayor Anderson, he's participated in a number of victories, including keeping high-level nuclear waste out of the state; supporting a ban on two sorts of low-level radioactive waste; forcing a toxic incinerator to eliminate 99 percent of its dioxin releases; and pressuring a magnesium refinery (arguably the dirtiest operation in America) to cut its toxic emissions by 95 percent. The list of achievements would be impressive even for a full-time environmental activist, but Ward is also a writer and a librarian. He's had help, he's quick to admit, mostly from exactly those stir-up-no-trouble rural Mormons who everybody told him were apathetic and cowed.

Twenty years ago Ward moved with his family to the flat salt plains an hour or so west of Salt Lake City and settled in Tooele County (pronounced *Too-willa*), where he ran the library's touring bookmobile. Traveling the area, he got to know its character and its characters: big, burly LDS men, for example, who'd testify in tears in church. "It's a patriotic place. Red-neck, blue-collar, white-trash. Emotional," Ward told me. "You don't tend to fight the hand that feeds you, that feeds your neighbor, and that feeds your neighbor's relatives." At the same time families are tight and very conscious of their history. "They have a lot of children, and organized geographically by church wards, they're very accustomed to working in groups." As an organizer, Ward could see the potential for collective action, as well as the pitfalls of closed-community conservative consciousness.

Some Utahans, no doubt, did fall in love with Reagan in 1980, but it didn't help Jimmy Carter that as president he approved a mobile-based nuclear missile system that would have torn up half of this state. Carter's madcap MX missile plan would have sucked up Utah's scarce water, eliminated thousands of acres of grazing land, and laced the place with miles of roads and rails—for starters. Then hundreds of seventy-foot-high, multiple-warhead nukes were supposed to travel around on those roads and rails in a fake-'em-out missile monte scheme that would have put a nuclear bull's-eye on Utah and neighboring Nevada. Utahans had already experienced life downwind from atomic fallout. A generation after the federal government conducted atmospheric nuclear bomb testing in Nevada in the 1950s, they witnessed cancer strike. (At the time of the testing, nearby Utahans were encouraged to set their chairs outside and watch the fun.) The LDS Church didn't like the Equal Rights Amendment, but neither did it like the sound of MX missiles. Ward formed an anti-MX coalition with his friends and neighbors and the local Catholic priest, but he's the first to admit that the LDS Church's formal statement in opposition was what scuttled the MX missile. Writes Ward, "Placing the heart of the Mormon population directly in the rocket sights of the Soviets didn't jive with existing revelation. . . . MX was dead meat."[5]

When we met in early 2006, Jason Groenewold was a handsome man in his late twenties whose tall, WASPy looks screamed "future congressman." He met Chip Ward when he was a ski bum straight out of college. In 2001 he became the director of HEAL Utah, an environmental organization that was founded with Chip Ward's help that year. A collection of Young Leader of the Year awards graced Groenewold's office wall. In five years Groenewold had turned an all-volunteer organization with no operational budget into a statewide alliance with three staff members and thousands of supporters. Asked for his secret, he replied: Don't attack people's opinions or leaders, if you want them on your side, and "don't make assumptions about people based on polling."

When Groenewold came to Utah from Madison, Wisconsin, in the late 1990s, most Utahans didn't even know that their state had a plan to dispose of nuclear waste. Polls taken over the previous couple of years showed in 2006 that 86 percent of the population knew, and they were against it. That kind of change doesn't happen in just a day, Groenewold told me over Mexican food at an excellent restaurant around the corner from his downtown Salt Lake office. It happens because people do a lot of work to get media attention and to get elected officials at high levels to speak out. "*Then* you take a poll. If someone had taken the poll at the start, we never would have engaged on this issue— we'd just have written it off as a loss to begin with," said Groenewold.

In comments directed to the Democratic Party's leaders in Washington, Groenewold said, "Years ago this state was Democratic. Someone on the other side decided they were going to dig in and build a base of support, and now they dominate the state. If we're just going to be cut out of the equation, then what's the point of being part of the United States? If you just say, 'Well, I can't get votes in Utah, so there's no point in doing anything for Utah,' you've really undermined a lot of people who are here. Just because someone rides in and gets the most votes doesn't mean they reflect the community. A lot of people just become disenchanted when they don't have someone speaking on their behalf."

Or when no one is speaking to them.

Much as pundits commonly attribute John Kerry's election defeat to his support for abortion and gay rights, Utahans have heard for years that the fight for the Equal Rights Amendment (ERA) "destroyed" their local Democratic Party. Jeff Bell, in the state party office, laid it out to me: "Our support of the ERA pretty much destroyed the Democratic Party in Utah." This convenient explanation puts the burden on "them," not on "us." *Look what we're up against,* it says—*inherently conservative people and an unmovable, irresistible church.* According to this way of thinking, whenever Democrats are too progressive, especially on those nasty "social" issues that touch people's personal lives, they lose. But just a few details are missing from this story. When Rocky Anderson looks at Utah history, he sees a state that was largely Democratic half a century ago. For that matter, it enfranchised women fifty years ahead of the federal government. Anderson looks at the records of three-term liberal governor Cal Rampton and of Senator Frank Moss, whose picture the mayor displays proudly on his desk. A liberal consumer advocate, Moss served eighteen years in the Utah senate (1959–77) and is the author of two prescient books: *The Water Crisis* (1967) and *Too Old, Too Sick, Too Bad: Nursing Homes in America* (1977).[6]

Moss would probably have won a fourth term if he hadn't been targeted by a fledging operation that was just then testing its wings: the New Right. In one of its earliest experiments in the use of targeted direct mail, phony think-tank "research," and sound-bite smear tactics, the New Right (led by Richard Viguerie, the Heritage Foundation, and their ilk) attacked Moss on behalf of Orrin Hatch, an antiunion, antiregulation, antiabortion conservative elected to the U.S. Senate in 1976. Had the Right followed the same reasoning that Democrats use today, they'd have gussied Orrin up in his best Consumers Union outfit to campaign as a just-slightly-tougher consumer advocate. Instead, corporate funders—including Adolph Coors—backed Hatch to take on an eighteen-year liberal incumbent by running as his exact opposite. And they won. Had Moss's constituents simply been making do with a liberal for eighteen years until someone conservative came along? It seems doubtful. More likely the Republicans knew that to change people's minds, you have to stir things up. You have to really pick a fight, not pick at it, squirm, and flinch.

In the 1970s, Lorna Vogt, deputy director of the Harm Reduction Project, a law-reform organization, was a teenager in Utah. At that time, the LDS elders were dead set against the ERA because it ran smack up against church patriarchy. (Lest we forget, the ERA would have outlawed discrimination against women, *period*.) LDS law considers all faithful Mormon males twelve years and older to be lay "priests," eligible for promotion to church leadership. Women may be leaders in auxiliary Relief Society Associations, but they are not ordained and are not eligible for positions in the priesthood hierarchy. In the early 1970s the church came out against the ERA and sent undercover "missionaries" across the country to defeat it. But lots of Mormons, including the Democratic governor at the time, Scott Matheson, supported the ERA. Sonia Johnson, a fifth-generation LDS mom who thought she should have at least the same rights as her sons, founded Mormons for ERA—and in 1979 was excommunicated for her trouble. One night when she was reading bedtime stories to her four children, two men knocked on her door with a summons to a church trial. Demonstrators chained themselves to the gates of the Salt Lake City Temple, and Mormon husbands "ordained" their wives in solidarity. Johnson arranged for a Mormons for ERA banner to soar over the LDS General Council.

Instead of building up support for the stirring groundswell behind Johnson, even pro-ERA Democrats beat a retreat. The ERA defeat excited Phyllis Schlafly and the others who had pioneered the fight. In the state-by-state strategy used to defeat the ERA, Schlafly saw a model she and her group, Eagle Forum, have used ever since. The one exception to the rule in Utah was Frances Farley, an outspoken feminist, well known for her support of abortion rights and the ERA, and her opposition to MX. In 1984 Farley ran for Congress against an incumbent Republican lieutenant governor and came within five hundred votes of winning, the tightest race of that year.

Lorna Vogt says liberals often think churches have more power than they actually do. Utah is the classic example. "It's convenient to see the LDS Church as this hulking monster, and in some ways it is," she says. "Politicians act as if they're speaking for it. Its power is hierarchical, top down, and effective. But I think some people use it as an excuse not to organize our own structures."

I met Vogt in 2006, in the week when the Senate Judiciary Committee in Washington was preparing to confirm to a lifetime appointment on the Supreme Court a man who approves of strip-searching ten-year-olds: a conservative jurist in the most antilibertarian sense, Samuel Alito. His judicial record was discussed mostly in terms of his opposition to *Roe v. Wade,* a legal decision that the majority of Americans favors. Less scrutinized was the judge's record as a soldier in the boondoggle War on Drugs, a massive incarceration and interception program that the majority of Americans, when polled, considers a dismal failure.

In Salt Lake City in January 2006, heartland Utahans are declaring the War on Drugs a disaster. In a crowded downtown auditorium on a Tuesday evening, hundreds of parents and friends of drug users file in for a meeting convened by Vogt and her colleague Luciano Colonna of the Salt Lake City–based Harm Reduction Project, a group calling for alternative approaches to overcoming drug addiction. "Sit anywhere," Vogt tells me, but finding a seat is not so easy. I settle in behind a warm, forty-something mom and dad who clutch each other's hands throughout the proceedings. "Our son's seventeen, and we're worried to death," the dad whispers to me during a break. Their son is attending a meeting for teens held simultaneously in a nearby building, learning concrete information about how to prevent deaths from drug overdose.

"Our policy makers have been going in absolutely the wrong direction," begins Mayor Rocky Anderson, just warming up. "Interdiction, source control, incarceration of millions of people. Half a million Americans are now in prison on offenses related to illegal drugs. It's expensive, it's harmful, and it doesn't work. If those programs had been successful, we'd have fewer drugs at higher prices. Instead we have the opposite. The War on Drugs has failed. We need to put money into programs that work instead."

It took me, a longtime New Yorker, a while to adjust to what I was hearing. In blue New York City, voters have been electing Republican mayors for years. The most famous is Rudolph Giuliani, who came to the job as a pro-cop city prosecutor after a stint in Reagan's Department of Justice. In New York, Giuliani resisted every effort to reform the state's draconian Rockefeller drug laws. As I sit in the Harm Reduction Project forum in Salt Lake, I realize that I'm not in Manhattan anymore: on the stage is not only the mayor but also the city prosecutor—both of whom are advocates of more sensible, treatment-based alternative sentencing and specially trained drug courts. Instead of throwing more and more nonviolent addicts into jail, they've overhauled the city's criminal justice system and replaced prison time with drug treatment. The professional expert witnesses include an infectious diseases specialist from New Mexico who says he was inspired by AIDS activists (who pioneered clean needle–exchange programs for intravenous drug users to stop them from using infected hypodermics).

The nonprofessional experts—and those who bring the house down—are the Mormon dads who talk about their dead sons.

"I lost my son Andrew when he was twenty-three. He was exciting and fun—and he was a heroin addict," begins one dad, Jack. Everyone knows the story. A series of overdose deaths had struck Salt Lake City recently. In 2004 a total of 190 Utahans had died from accidental drug overdose. The drug involved in the fastest-growing group of cases is illegal—crystal meth—but the largest group uses nonillicit drugs like methadone, OxyContin, and hydrocodone. More than one teen died while his friends panicked, not daring to call 911 for fear that instead of an ambulance, cops would arrive, arrest them, and send them away for life. The Harm Reduction Project's director, Luciano Colonna, made one point repeatedly during the evening: such deaths could be prevented if the victims and other people present had the skills and information about how to respond—that is, if they were not terrified literally to death by the War on Drugs.

When Peter Philips speaks, the place becomes especially quiet. Peter's story is haunting, and he doesn't get through telling it without choking up. He did everything he could think of to punish, protect, and push his nineteen-year-old to stay in treatment, but like most addicted people, his kid kept crashing, failing again and again to receive effective help. Peter's son had died just a few months earlier in horrible circumstances, in the presence of his fiancée, who didn't dare make a phone call.

"My son is now ashes in a jar in a closet in his bedroom," says Philips through his tears. "I want a second chance to save someone else's son."

Call it broken-heartland America; Democrats are living in a bubble if they think there's any excuse not to confront this stuff. Those scary "social" issues like policing, discriminating, and parenting aren't deadly politically; they're deadly. And if you can talk about them with parents, prosecutors, professionals, and politicians *in Utah,* you can talk about them anywhere.

The last weekend I'm in Utah, I attend a lobbying session by the gay group Equality Utah, at the capitol. The group's number one goal is to pass a hate crimes bill that for fifteen years has failed in the state legislature, and to stop a proposed ban on high school gay-straight clubs. Some 180 LGBT activists and allies are briefed by the two out gay members of Utah's state legislature, Jackie Biskupski and Scott McCoy. In 1998 Representative Biskupski won election by a two-to-one margin in spite of an antihomosexual ad campaign financed by the Eagle Forum. A lesbian activist and the first out legislator in state history, Biskupski has been reelected three times to her Salt Lake City district. McCoy was a leader in the fight against Amendment 3, the Utah antigay marriage amendment. When a seat in his district became vacant midterm, he lobbied party delegates and went on to win an upset nomination to fill the empty seat.

"Democracy's not a spectator sport," McCoy told the lobbyists-in-training. In the weeks that followed, their lobbying paid off. On the last day of the legislative session, over the complaints of the state's most conservative senator, Chris Buttars, Utah legislators finally passed the hate crimes law. And Buttars's proposed ban on gay-straight clubs in high schools never even came up for a vote. In fact, only one of the five bills that Equality Utah opposed passed, and that measure—which would have blocked courts granting caretaking rights to nonbiological families—was vetoed by the governor, Jon Huntsman Jr. (a Mormon Republican). In 2006 Biskupski and McCoy won reelection, and they were joined by a third out legislator—a progressive, Christine Johnson—who defeated a more conservative Democrat in a primary race for an open seat and went on to win 75–25 in a strongly Democratic district.

When cinema owner Larry Miller canceled the screening of *Brokeback Mountain*, pundits and late-night comics in New York and Los Angeles salivated over yet another example of bigotry in what actor Heath Ledger called America's "hostile heartland." But the striking news from Utah, it seemed to me, wasn't that one conservative business owner behaved predictably but that in an indisputably conservative environment, far more diversity was thriving than the conventional wisdom allowed for. Miller censored *Brokeback Mountain* at a handful of suburban malls, but in downtown Salt Lake, the film was playing on five other screens to sold-out audiences. On opening night in Provo, quite possibly the most conservative place in the country, people were lining up to see the boots-and-butts romance just down Main Street from Brigham Young (dubbed "breed 'em young") University, the world headquarters of the LDS Church. That Friday night the cinema was full, and the happy-looking students sporting tight-fitting jeans and meticulous sideburns didn't look so different from the audiences in New York City's Greenwich Village.

Shortly before his assassination in 1963, John F. Kennedy toured the western states. Speaking in Billings, Montana, at an event slated to focus on environmental protection, the president strayed off message and mentioned the just-signed U.S.-Soviet nuclear test ban treaty. The audience's response was far more enthusiastic than Kennedy had expected, and so he carried on talking about the test ban treaty as he traveled around the West. The last stop of his tour was Salt Lake City. Kennedy entered the Mormon Tabernacle, "allegedly the enemy camp," where a five-minute standing ovation greeted him. David Halberstam, in *The Best and the Brightest*, writes:

Here again, in what was alleged to be Birch country, Goldwater territory, he challenged the theses of the far right and talked of the problem of living in a complicated world. He had long suspected that the right in America was overrated as a political force, that there was an element of blackmail to its power, and now he was convinced that the country was going past old and rigid fears of the Communists, that it was probably ahead of Washington in its comprehension of the world and its willingness to accept it (and if not ahead of Washington, at least far ahead of where Washington thought it was). He sensed that there was a deep longing for a sane peace and sane world.[7]

Since 1963, and even since Halberstam's book was published in 1972, the Right has had a huge impact on national and state politics, and Utah is not a bad state to see how the story has played out. In 2001 Utah's second congressional district was captured for Democrats by Jim Matheson, son of the popular two-term governor. Matheson is a man who fits the Brigham Young recommendations to a tee: he voted to abrogate Congress's power to wage war by giving George W. Bush a blank slate to invade Iraq; he voted for the USA Patriot Act, for a "marriage amendment" to the U.S. Constitution, and for the so-called late-term-abortion ban; he supported the Central America Free Trade Agreement and the elimination of the estate tax; and he voted yes on bankruptcy reform, which has made it harder for poor and middle-class people to declare bankruptcy, even though Utahans (with their large families and their mandatory 10 percent tithes to the church) file for bankruptcy more than residents of any other state.

Matheson's a nice enough guy, Mayor Anderson tells me, "but in terms of Democratic values, what have we won?" he asks. Does the mayor wish he'd dodged that gay marriage question in 1996? No. He believes he helped move the issue forward. Ten years later, four U.S. senators (Wyden, Feingold, Kennedy, and Chafee) had come out for marriage equality. Changes don't happen if people don't push, he concludes. Meanwhile, as mayor, Anderson's been able to test policies in ways that other officials can't. At a time when Democrats are constantly accused of having few fresh proposals, he's actually been able to try out ideas and develop successful programs (like the light rail system) that are now being adopted in Salt Lake and Davis counties, which until recently were sternly opposed.

While conservatives lock down policy formation at the national level, cities serve as crucibles where progressives versed in what Halberstam calls the details of "a complicated world" can have a voice. At a time when government in general is under assault, progressive cities can provide a sense of hope and possibility. If the federal and state levels are cut off, the city may be the last place where things can actually happen. City mayors can even inspire. Many say that the way Salt Lake City has thrived under Mayor Anderson helped elect Peter Corroon, a cousin of Howard Dean, mayor of Salt Lake County, in the 2004 general election. Half the population of Utah lives in Salt Lake County. They're now led by a pretty liberal Democrat. In July 2005, Rocky Anderson issued an executive order requiring that all new city buildings adopt energy efficiency programs and cut down on pollution. Nine months later Peter Corroon did the same thing. There's power in numbers. Removed from the context of political campaigns, even those hot-button issues can lose their sting. Some 249 of the Fortune 500 companies offer health and other benefits to the same-sex partners of their employees. (That's up from just 28 a decade ago.) More than 80 percent ban discrimination on the basis of sexual orientation. "A lot of people in the business community see progressives as being really healthy for economic development," Mayor Anderson adds. "They know that the view of Utah as backward, bigoted, and homogenous isn't good for our state." Anderson uses his office as mayor to make the case that the state's conservative reputation is bad for business.

"Utah's not the outback colony of cowboys and cult members that people seem to think we are," Gena Edvalson, one of Reverend Dennison's congregants in Salt Lake City, told me at a trendy "fair trade" coffee shop near her office. Edvalson is the executive director of the Utah Progressive Network.

"People don't believe progressive Utahans even exist. I like to say we're Utah's best-kept secret," Edvalson continued. After all, the election-night map of Utah isn't wrong at the level of party affiliation, she says. But in the daily lives of people, the blue and red lines are more blurred. It takes a lot to change a Utahan's party identification, Edvalson admits, but people form opinions and beliefs about issues based on experience, she says, and those experiences can add nuance to even the most conservative voters' views. When they let their principles drive their politics rather than the other way around, progressives stand to win victories that are worth fighting for, even if they take years to achieve. And along the way, engaging, rather than ducking, the tough debates pays rewards.

Gena Edvalson chose to engage rather than duck when she moved back to her native Salt Lake City from California. "People from outside Utah are shocked when they hear I come from an LDS family and live in a conservative suburb of Salt Lake. They're even more shocked when they find out that I'm a lesbian, that I have a partner who is about to have a kid, and that my father, who is eighty-three years old and very Mormon, lives in the house with us."

Gena and her partner, Jana, drop Mr. Edvalson off at his church on Sundays, on their way to South Valley Unitarian. "I don't have the luxury of painting everyone as a horrible Republican because that would be most everyone I know," says Edvalson, on the walk from her local coffee shop back to the office. "All the neighbors know. We're incredibly out," she continues. Aren't those neighbors the people who voted for a gay marriage ban in 2004? I ask. Yes, she replies, but one defeat is no reason to give up the fight. When a storm hit town a few years back, a neighbor showed up with a chainsaw to clear Gena's lawn, unasked. "They're not horrible homophobic people who'd run us out of the neighborhood. They just don't realize that through legislation they're doing essentially that. It's our responsibility to communicate."

In 2004 Gena and Jana put up a sign on their lawn against Amendment 3, the anti–gay marriage initiative. They didn't think the sign would sway people's votes, but they knew it would lead to conversations. It did. "I understand Mormon culture better than I really want to. I know exactly what they're being told and how that's influencing their behavior at the polls," Edvalson explains. "But they can't keep hold of that when they're dealing with us personally." On Election Day Gena, Jana, Gena's dad, and Maureen (a woman about his age who lives next door) went to the polls together. After voting, the group returned home, and along the way Maureen confided that she'd voted against the amendment.

It's not as if Maureen represented the majority—the amendment, which passed with 66 percent of the vote, had the LDS Church's full weight—and untold dollars—behind it. But the outcome wasn't a total disaster. (The Right had assumed that the anti-amendment side would lose by an 80–20 wipeout.) By Edvalson's account, it was a forward loss. Progressives in many red states talk about "losing forward." It's the notion that you can end up ahead of where you started—even if you lose, because during the fight you pick up allies. "Our job is to build bridges to potential allies," says Gena. If you won't go near the water, it's hard to build a bridge.

Montana Miracle

CHAPTER THREE ☆ # Workers

"Section 1. Popular sovereignty. All political power is vested in and derived from the people. All government of right originates with the people, is founded upon their will only, and is instituted solely for the good of the whole."

—The Constitution of the State of Montana, as adopted by the Constitutional Convention, March 22, 1972, and ratified by the people, June 6, 1972

At six foot two and a burly 205 pounds, Brian Schweitzer is a big guy from the Big Sky State, but he's not all that is going on in Montana. The agronomist from Whitefish burst onto the national political scene in November 2004, when Montanans elected him governor, the first Democrat to hold the office since 1988. Even as Bush/Cheney trounced Kerry/Edwards in their state, Montana Democrats regained power in the state house after twelve years of Republican majorities and sparked breathless talk about a "Montana miracle" that might be a model for Democratic success across the

West, if only the party could take a tip or two from Schweitzer. Two years later, Democratic congressional candidates were cozying up to Schweitzer with all the alacrity that some Republicans were fleeing their president.

I flew into Missoula in early March 2006 with a clipping file full of hyperbole. *Rolling Stone* magazine called Schweitzer the nation's "hottest governor." "The future is wearing a turquoise bolo tie wrapped around the collar of a blue and white striped, button-down dress shirt," began an article in the online magazine *Salon*. Stretching to convey the Montana governor's home-on-the-ranch charm, a *New York Times* journalist worked pesticide, mold, and saliva into a single sentence: "The Democratic governor-elect, Brian Schweitzer, is a rancher who knows fertilizer from fungus and can spit and talk health care at the same time." Another journalist summed up the consensus: "Schweitzer single-handedly trounced the Republican Party."

When CBS's *60 Minutes* interviewed Schweitzer about his plan to synthesize diesel fuel from coal, Lesley Stahl dubbed him the "coal cowboy." The blogosphere has been just as thrilled. The Howard Deaniacs at DailyKos.com have another sleeves-rolled-up governor to love: the blogger Markos, or "Kos," dubbed Schweitzer "Howard Dean on the ranch." Author-activist David Sirota, who took time off from a job at the Center for American Progress to work on Schweitzer's campaign, put it this way: "The story begins with the man himself," he wrote. "If you look in an encyclopedia under 'Montana: Self-Image of,' you'll find a picture of Brian Schweitzer."

When we arranged to broadcast my radio show live from the party's annual Mansfield-Metcalf Dinner (a pep rally for the Montana Democratic Party), Schweitzer had been in office for more than a year, but the evening still felt like the governor's prom night. The charming stained-glass civic center in the breezy gold-mining town of Helena was packed with six hundred donors and candidate hopefuls. When the speeches were over, a Native American drumming band performed, and there was live dancing, but even those who found the festivities distracting had no trouble focusing on Brian Schweitzer. When veteran Montana senator Max Baucus tried to lead the crowd in a chorus of "We Can Do Better," it was all call, no response. When Schweitzer took the stage even for a moment, he commanded the full attention of the crowd. It's refreshing to see a man in a blue denim shirt and jeans address a stuffy party dinner as governor, and it's even more refreshing when he's accompanied not by his campaign consultant, but by his border collie, Jag.

"There is nothing but excitement here. Montana Democrats are on a roll," Schweitzer said as soon as he sat down with me. The big man in the denim certainly seems to be basking in a glow. In six short years he's gone from a career in agricultural science, working contracts in Libya and the United Arab Emirates, to a long-shot (near-win) bid to unseat Republican senator Conrad Burns in 2000, to a barnstorming tour through every part of Montana and a victory on November 2, 2004, the very night John Kerry and John Edwards went down to defeat. Now Schweitzer's seen as a great hope for western Democrats and maybe for Democrats everywhere. Within fifty-four days of coming into office—his first-ever elected position—he was selected to deliver the Democrats' weekly radio address.

For all the excitement, there's remarkably little consensus over just what pulled off the 2004 "Montana miracle." Observers can find something in Schweitzer to applaud wherever they stand politically. Ex-Republicans praise his selection of Republican state senator John Bohlinger as his running mate, and right-wing Democrats credit him with reaching so-called cultural conservatives by speaking to their values around small government and guns. "He's as much a prairie centrist as a prairie populist," Bruce Reed of the DLC told the *New York Times*. Liberals admire him for bucking the DLC party line on NAFTA and Iraq and talking a blue streak about energy conservation; he also supports a woman's right to choose. "Schweitzer is emblematic of a new kind of western politician who is both progressive and entrepreneurial," wrote *The American Prospect*'s Robert Kuttner.

Seemingly starstruck, Kos and his coauthor Jerome Armstrong describe Schweitzer as a kind of Democratic dragon slayer who not only ousted the GOP, but vanquished what the bloggers consider the irksome "issue groups" within the Democratic Party. Referring to women's groups, environmentalists, and labor, Kos and Armstrong wrote approvingly in their book, *Crashing the Gate*, that "Montana Democrats nearly cut the issue groups out of their campaign efforts." The bloggers alleged that Schweitzer "threw all the interest group questionnaires in the garbage." Which proved, in their view, that "Schweitzer and the rest of the Democratic ticket in Montana could stand on their own, unencumbered by whatever negative baggage those groups might bring."

It's our favorite version of history: how one man did it, how he beat the odds. But it's not how politics works and it's certainly not what happened in Montana. To talk about a one-man miracle is to see only the beaming baby and ignore the nine months and Mom. As two local feminists, Judy Smith and Terry Kendrick, put it in their essay, "Revisiting the Montana Miracle," "Rather than a 'miracle' it was more like a perfect storm." What is happening in Montana may have lessons for national Democrats, but not if the analysis starts and stops with Schweitzer and his boots and bolo.

"That so-called miracle—it took us ten years to pull that off," says Bill Lombardi, a longtime Democratic consultant in Montana. It's not very miraculous what happened here, he continues, except in the sense that Montana Democrats, written off by their national counterparts, went their own way and did things—successfully—that the national party has refused to do. It wasn't the work of one year or even one very good candidate; it was the result of twelve years spent building up the state party infrastructure and forging relationships between the party and key community organizations.

It will take a whole lot more than a trip to the western-wear store to mimic what happened in Montana. This is a massive state—the size of Germany—with a population still under a million (around 900,000). With numbers that small even tiny constituencies, well organized, can tip the balance (as Montanans found again, in the elections of 2006). One group of unsung miracle workers in Montana were Native Americans, who make up roughly 7 percent of the population. After years of fighting vote suppression of minority voters, redistricting created more native districts, and a vigorous registration drive produced more native voters—more than 80 percent of them voting Democratic. Redistricting helped, as did a decade of GOP extremism. (In 2004 one former GOP chair urged fellow Republicans to vote for Schweitzer, and another GOP county party split, with moderates issuing press releases about their party's having been "hijacked by extremists.") Schweitzer's predecessor's approval numbers scratched 18 percent before she quit. His opponent, Secretary of State Bob Brown, was outspent, $620,000 to $540,000, by Schweitzer.

In contrast to their colleagues in other states, the Montana Democratic Party didn't rely on paid workers flown in from out of state to get out the vote on Election Day. Brad Martin, director of the state party's coordinated campaign, deployed a home-state staff and fielded close to three thousand local volunteers, and Martin, a former community organizer with the Public Interest Research Group (PIRG), wasn't the only one with ground troops. Women's groups, conservationists, and other nonprofits got involved in the election of 2004 as never before. They helped drive up turnout from 60 to 71 percent. Brian Schweitzer wasn't the only beneficiary. Montana Democrats won three out of four statewide races and made a clean sweep of almost every statewide office. They picked up five seats, fighting to a 50–50 tie in the assembly and won a 27–23 majority in the senate. Although voters approved an anti–gay marriage initiative, they also legalized medical marijuana, sustained a ban on a particularly noxious type of mining, and raised tobacco taxes. While John Kerry lost to Bush by twenty points, Schweitzer beat Brown by 224,506 votes to Brown's 204,863.

A wry smile comes to Pat Williams's face when I ask him about the buzz surrounding the new man in the governor's mansion. Williams represented Montana in the U.S. Congress from 1979 to 1996—nine terms—the longest-serving congressman in U.S. history. If it takes rumors of a miracle to get people to pay attention to Montana, that's okay with Williams. "I think we have as fine-tuned a coalition of liberal partnerships in Montana as probably exists anywhere." It's about time people gave Montana a second look, he says. "Why is it that people are still calling Montana a red state? The facts don't support it." As he sits in his Missoula office, a renovated railway station that has been turned into the Center for the Study of the Rocky Mountain West, Williams's conversation jumps from the Montana history that is depicted on his walls to Montanans he grew up with—including Evel Knievel, the great motorcycle stuntman from Butte—and the men he served with in Congress. The two most famous, after whom the party's annual dinner is named, are U.S. senators Lee Metcalf and Mike Mansfield. "Here's this senator, Mike, who was majority leader longer than anybody in history, a liberal, and after Mike, I served this state for eighteen years." Metcalf was an early advocate for wilderness protection; Mansfield, who turned against the Vietnam War, introduced the 1964 Civil Rights Act. The party never seemed interested in how Mansfield and Metcalf, and after them Williams, won office. "They didn't really give much of a damn," Williams says and sighs. When he was in Congress, whenever he offered advice to the Democratic National Committee or the campaign committees, he was rebuffed. "I was elected nine times. They acted like it was some quirk, inexplicable, when in fact there were in-gredients," he points out.

Like the rest of the nation, Montana didn't simply "swing" to the right. It was pushed, by a well-financed GOP that saw potential for power in the region, and an organized movement of the extreme Right that used violence and threats of violence to intimidate the opposition. Ronald Reagan did well out here; in 1984 the West had grown enough in population to command 111 electoral votes (30 percent more than in 1960), making it a presidential prize worth winning. While Democratic leaders looked away, the Right honed in. With every electoral victory around the country, the GOP sent more cash westward, and the conser-vative movement targeted Montanans with messages that were well de-signed to split the Democratic coalition. Government liberals have gone too far, they said: they've corrupted your kids and regulated you out of a job. Alongside the party message came a more extreme version, articulated by overtly racist and Nazi groups. In the late 1980s, groups like the Militia of Montana started holding training meetings in the Montana Rockies. Over the same period, corporate-backed, antienvi-ronmentalist Wise Use activists began heckling government regulators in public meetings. In 1992 the Christian Coalition and the conservative American Family Association teamed up to take down the last progres-sive Democrat, with symbolic significance on the national as well as the Montana scene. The Christian Coalition's Ralph Reed flew to Mon-tana for a conference at which he called on fundamentalists to use stealth tactics to win political office. Reed summoned what he called "God's Army" specifically to defeat Pat Williams. "If we move forward in unity and if we will be persistent, victory will be ours . . . in Mon-tana . . . all across America." The pretext was Williams's role chairing the congressional committee that defended the National Endowment for the Arts against censorship. Williams fought back, challenging the coalition's tax-exempt status, and held on to office long enough to retire in 1996. But the attack on Williams was just a start.

Ken Toole, who monitored meetings of groups like the Militia of Montana, recalls that just as American liberals today tend to dismiss Bush backers as dim or deluded, "everyone wanted to think the haters were all crazy or led by the nose by some outsider." From what he saw at meetings, "it was the ideas that attracted them and the ideas that held them together." In a period of shrinking employment in Montana's traditional industries (mining and timber) and shrinking government programs in the area of education or training, the Right's ideas—mostly scapegoating environmentalists, queers, immigrants, feminists, and the poor—were the only ones out there. By the mid-1990s, with the Democrats' having all but abandoned the field, the various strains of the Right were ruling the roost with almost no ideological resistance.

In 1994 Montana Democrats found themselves in the same fix that national Democrats woke up to in 2002: out of office in both houses of the legislature and in the governor's mansion. "We were out in the wilderness, lost, and trying to figure out why we were lost," Democratic consultant Bill Lombardi told me. From a comfortably Democratic state that had in its history returned only one Republican to the Senate, Montana's numbers had shifted by the early 1990s, and a whole lot of traditional Democratic voters (women, blue-collar workers, low-income urban dwellers) had dropped out of the process or abandoned the state, or the Democratic Party altogether. In 1994, the year that swept Newt Gingrich to power in the U.S. Congress, Montana Democrats won only 33 out of 100 seats in the state assembly and 19 out of 50 in the state senate. The reasons were partly demographics: working-class miners and timber industry workers had moved out; middle-class retirees and urban whites in flight from the coasts had moved in. But liberals were also demonized by an organized right-wing campaign.

"The Christian Coalition and the Wise Use movement drove wedges into our base," says Lombardi. At that point Montana Democrats did something the national Democrats are just beginning to do. "We had to figure out how to communicate more effectively about what we stand for," he says. Twelve years ahead of Howard Dean's Fifty-State Strategy, Montana Democrats conducted their own internal review of the state party's infrastructure. The party held a statewide retreat and launched what was, in Lombardi's telling, an "offensive" that entailed the then-unusual practice (at the state and national levels) of Democratic elected officials actually meeting with one another on a regular basis and with outsiders. For the first time in the state party's history, Democratic leaders of the legislature met regularly with statewide officials and local party activists. "Two thousand and four wasn't a victory built into one electoral cycle. It has been built, built, built," Lombardi stresses.

The Democratic Party conventionally posits a choice between "broadening the electorate" (which usually means dashing for Republican voters) and "deepening the natural base" (which often means talking to groups the party's never talked to or hasn't talked to in years). It's a false choice, and in Montana, Democrats did both. They made some of the changes out of their own free will, but others were pushed upon them by the state's biggest minority, Native Americans. Montana has more Native American reservations than any other state (seven), and it is also home to more tribes (eleven). Indians make up only a small percentage of Montana's population, but in some districts, and on the reservations, they are a 90 percent majority. Until very recently, voting registration and turnout among Indians have been low; even in places where they were in the majority few registered, and Democrats paid the price because native voters tend to vote Democratic almost as solidly as African Americans do—roughly 80 percent vote blue. Reservations were potential blue dots in rural parts of Montana but only when Natives voted.

"We have felt powerless, and we've been told that we are powerless," says state representative Carol Juneau, who grew up on a reservation and lives today on the Blackfeet Reservation in northern Montana. Native people have their own elected tribal leaders. It's taken local activists years, says Juneau, to build any sense of engagement in non-native politics. Besides, state authorities—and politicians of both parties—have actively worked to keep Indians *out* of the process. Until the 1980s, even counties like Big Horn, with heavily native populations (46 percent), had never elected a native person to county or statewide office. When Natives did enter races, as four did in 1982—a Democratic primary—non-Indian Democrats accused them of cheating.[1]

In Montana simply leveling the playing field required redistricting. (The opportunity arises once every decade.) It also meant standing up to the structural racism that suppressed the Native American vote. When Democrats took back the statehouse in 2004, Republicans in Montana cried foul and blamed partisanship in the redistricting process. But the redistricting that took place in 2003 wasn't determined by either party; it was determined by Janine Pease Pretty on Top, a well-known Native American leader whom the Montana Supreme Court appointed chair of the redistricting committee. The final plan created several more competitive districts across the state, and three more constituencies—two in the Senate and one in the House—in which Native Americans represent a majority.

Instead of conducting outreach to minority voters and dismissing those who failed to participate, Montana Democrats gave enough resources directly to local Native American leaders that they could participate on an equal footing and build their own base. "[To start,] we gave that money to a virtually all-white, all-male consulting group in Helena. . . . They didn't consult. The effort collapsed," says Pat Williams, who worked vigorously on the Native American issue in the late 1990s. He saw to it that get-out-the-vote, or GOTV, money went directly to the reservations. In 2004, over the objections of his political staff, funding went to the local native leadership. "I was assured by everybody that the Indians would drink the money. Instead they had the highest gain of any ethnic group in any state in registration and turnout."

In 2004 the coordinated campaign of the Montana Democratic Party hired a Democratic Party tribal coordinator. On each reservation voters were registered, and local candidates were recruited. By Election Day an estimated four thousand new voters—about 10 percent of the reservation voting population—were newly registered, and more were running for office. The delegation sent to Helena after the 2004 election included eight Native Americans (the second highest number of native legislators in any state), all of them Democrats. The lowest turnout of registered voters on any reservation was 49 percent; in some places turnout exceeded 80 percent of all voting-age Native Americans.

The Right's rhetoricians appealed to one populist tradition in Montana, but populism comes in many flavors. The Reagan Republicans and their allies emphasized the mythic go-it-alone spirit of pioneers. (In fact, pioneers got a whole lot of help from federal troops and government-paid-for railroads.) Progressives draw on an equally populist western tradition, of citizens' not going alone, but coming together. In the nineteenth century, Butte, Montana, was the most solidly unionized town in the United States. Photographs of Butte's Labor Day march in the 1890s show union bands and banners pouring like a river from one end of town to the other.

By the early twentieth century, big business (mostly the mining and timber corporations) had tamed the unions and almost literally bought up the government. The massive Butte-based Anaconda Copper Company (which once produced a quarter of the world's supply of copper) didn't have to worry about public relations; it owned every newspaper (except the Communist Party paper), and the company's bagman took what would today be called campaign contributions to the state legislature every week. In the 1960s, with the rise of environmentalism (probably the most influential popular movement after organized labor in this state), pressure grew for Montanans to take their government back and save their state from environmental ruin. By referendum, voters called for the rewriting of their state constitution. In 1972 one hundred delegates (with just one thing in common, that they weren't politicians) hashed out a document that established new rights, among them the right to a "clean and healthful environment," and the right to public participation in government. Citizen delegates established a constitutional right to personal privacy (which feminists hope defends abortion rights in their state), and a provision that recognizes the contribution of Native Americans to Montana history.

Dorothy Eck, the delegate who fought for what's known as the Indian education provision in the constitution (a requirement that public schools teach everyone about Native American history), believes to this day that the greatest outcome of what was called the ConCon was the sense it gave to regular Montanans that they had a right, and a responsibility, to be involved in their government.

"We opened the process up to everybody by putting little ads in the paper. People could write down recommendations of what they thought should be in the constitution. And every suggestion was considered," Eck, now in her nineties, was a delegate to Montana's 1972 Constitutional Convention. It was, in her words, "a great convening."

A "convening" is not a bad word to describe what's happening in Montana again. The day I arrive in Missoula, I meet a bright, blond activist named Betsy Hands. As we drive around town, she tells me she is a former Peace Corps volunteer and an environmental scientist who has spent years in various African countries; she also once led trips for the wilderness camp Outward Bound. She is program director at Home-

WORD, a community housing organization that helps low-income women acquire cheap mortgaged housing. She's also a competitive telemark skier, and oh yes, she's running for the state assembly. "Somebody's got to step up, and why not me?" Hands tells me cheerfully. It's an attitude I hear a lot in Montana.

On March 8, International Women's Day, at the Missoula Women's Day Potluck, trestle tables sag under the array of food. A cheerful noise spurts through from a child care room next door. Around the hall women's groups working on violence, health care, and workplace discrimination are scattered about. What these groups have in common, I gradually learn, is that they are all part of something called Montana Women Vote, a coalition of ten statewide women's organizations focused on increasing women's participation in elections and encouraging women to run for office. This isn't a presidential election season, and it's eight months before a congressional midterm race, yet on just about every table there is something about voting, a flyer about a candidate's fund-raiser, or an invitation to attend a candidate's training. Sheets of talking points on various issues are in good supply, and voter registration forms are abundant.

"The thing I often say about electoral politics is that I never thought I'd find myself doing it," Judy Smith tells me. Smith is a longtime activist and cofounder with Terry Kendrick of Montana Women Vote. In the mid-1990s the Democratic Party was not alone in being fed up with losing to the Right: issue groups were too. Montana feminists have a rich history to draw on, as the state was the first to send a woman to Congress, in 1916—Jeannette Rankin, a pacifist who voted against both world wars. Fifty-three percent of Montanans say they are pro-choice. When I sit down for dinner with Smith and Kendrick, we are eating pizza above a Jeannette Rankin Peace Center, while a clump of picketers organized by Planned Parenthood gather not far away, protesting the nomination of Samuel Alito to the Supreme Court.

"I was part of that radical contingent in the 1960s and 1970s that thought electoral politics was not something that would make real change," Smith tells me. Her beliefs haven't changed that much, she says, but the possibility of affecting policy-makers through movement pressure, like street demonstrations, did. By the late 1990s, local women's groups like HomeWORD could not muster enough power to match the corporate campaign controllers, developers, and the bullyboys of the Christian Right. Besides, they had no allies to lobby in the state-house. Instead of simply railing from a distance about a cowed Democratic establishment, Smith and Kendrick decided to do something. "Instead of running into that wall over and over, we had to crack that wall open," she explains. And others felt that way as well.

Low-income women and minorities were not the only Montanans who were sick and tired of being sidelined and stonewalled in state government in the 1990s. If the politicians weren't going to put up a fight, conservationists too decided they had to take up politics. After the 1972 constitution established a right to a "clean and healthful environment," the state passed a series of forward-looking laws, regulating emissions and preserving park land. During the years of Republican dominance, those laws took a pounding from the Right. The state energy company was deregulated. Dams were privatized. "Our laws had been gutted, and just working on lobbying and rulemaking wasn't enough. We realized we had to change the policy-makers, and that demanded a political response. We had to elect people," Theresa Keaveny, executive director of Montana Conservation Voters, tells me. MCV is a statewide membership organization of some forty thousand Montanans that does electoral work through an affiliated political action committee, or PAC. Get-out-the-vote and voter-registration work is done through its sister nonprofit, the MCV Education Fund.

The most active PAC in the state in 2004, the Montana Conservation Voters PAC, spent $224,000 in state races, and $76,000 on the governor's race—the largest independent expenditure by any group. MCV didn't just give, Keaveny and her colleagues consulted with candidates—and with voters. Well in advance of the 2004 election, MCV bought public voting files, broken down by precinct, and compiled voter guides of legislators' voting records on conservation issues. Since the election, MCV has kept a running scorecard of legislators' conservation-related votes. "It's our job to get [our base] engaged and thinking straight about using their own power to keep politicians accountable," says Keaveny. Her passion for data-mining is contagious. Over breakfast in a Helena coffee shop, she pulls out chart after chart. She says she's able to sit down with candidates and, drawing on polling, talk to them about the opinions of people in their districts. "We provide more than the party does, because we break it out by precinct and show the green voter strength. We also show the voting propensity, so people can make good decisions about their strategy.... We are able to be quite persuasive." She grins.

Although they can't (and don't) endorse specific candidates, non-profits like MCV and Montana Women Vote (MWV) can conduct low-cost, high-impact voter-registration drives that reach key parts of the electorate that candidates miss. Nationally, polls show that only about 30 percent of low-income women register to vote, let alone show up at the polls. Officially, Democrats know that low-income women are a target group, but at the state level few parties have the resources—or the networks—to do the work of turning those voters out. In 2004 the ten member groups of Montana Women Vote, which work on women's issues year-in and year-out, set a target of registering five thousand new voters, especially low-income women in certain districts. They ended up registering 7,300 new voters. MWV borrowed files from Keaveny and learned how to cross-reference voting records with their own membership lists. "This isn't rocket science," says Judy Smith.

Pooling their resources, Montana Women Vote volunteers contacted voters not once or twice but several times and distributed voter guides. After Election Day, Kendrick was able to look at the MWV list and compare it to the voter file. Seventy-seven percent of the MWV registrants voted—a rate 6 percent *higher* than the statewide turnout. In its first year MWV alone turned out 5,621 new, disproportionately Democratic voters. Thanks to sophisticated tracking software, Theresa Keaveny was able to show that where the MCV was active, turnout was 14 to 19 percent higher than average: 84 percent of its registrants voted, as did 93 percent of its own members—a minimum of thirty thousand votes. In a gubernatorial race that was decided by just 19,700 votes, those numbers were huge.

Movement activists didn't just turn out voters, they also ran for office, some for their second or third terms. "Someone had to provide an ideological foil to the Right, if only to put some brakes on those guys, or put little speed bumps in their road," says Ken Toole, whose roots in Montana history go back a century. His father was a state historian, the founder of the Historical Museum; a Toole was the state's first governor. To monitor and respond to hate groups, Toole and his colleague Christine Kaufmann founded the Montana Human Rights Network in the late 1980s. By 2000 they had decided they had to do more than agitate. Sometimes the most important question is not "Can you win?" but "Can you provide an alternative and use a campaign to advance a message?" "That's what the Right has done for decades. They run not to win, but to campaign," Toole told me when we met.

Montana is a state where a little money goes a long, long way. Most legislative campaigns there cost a maximum of about $10,000. In 2000 Toole and Kaufmann took leave from their nonprofit jobs to run for the legislature—Toole in the state senate, Kaufmann in the state house. Both won. An out lesbian (the second in the Montana legislature), Kaufmann ran in a district that includes not only a Catholic college but also a cathedral. Against all the odds, she beat three other Democrats in the primary and then won against her Republican opponent, a well-connected fundraiser for Catholic Charities. She's been reelected ever since. In 2006 Toole, term-limited out of the senate, ran for a seat on the Public Services Commission, which regulates energy utilities. In the race he faced off with his opponent over the issue of energy deregulation. Energy deregulation, he argued, had brought Montana from having some of the lowest consumer energy prices to the highest. "Public debates are the best way for voters to get the information they need," Toole told the press.

Raising money through their affiliated PACs, both the conservation voters and the women's groups have begun recruiting people to run in primaries. Keaveny's Montana Conservation Voters PAC targeted nine candidates to support in 2004; six won. Judy Smith formed a "Take Montana Back" PAC that backed progressive Democrats, including Kaufmann, Toole, and Mary Caferro, a single mother and former welfare recipient who directs the antipoverty organization WEEL (Working for Equality and Economic Liberation), a member group of the Montana Women Vote coalition.

"I'm a low-income, single, working parent with four kids and a job. I know how to multitask," laughs Caferro. With sparkling blue eyes and wispy black hair that cascades down her back, she's about a quarter the size of Brian Schweitzer but she matches his energy, spark for spark. She's slight in the style of Loretta Lynn, the coalminer's daughter—which is to say, a powerhouse. She had a lot of reasons to run, she tells me in her office, way too late one Friday night in Helena. One was to give people a reason to believe in government. "I was afraid that if we had another Republican majority, the last programs for low-income Montanans would be cut, and that would give poor people all the more reason to be discouraged and get alienated. I wanted people to see me and say: if Mary Caferro can run and win, I have a reason to continue to be part of the process." MCV provided the data on Caferro's district; Kaufmann and Toole mentored the first-time candidate. She ran against a well-connected conservative incumbent and won, 65 to 35. Then she knocked on doors every day until Election Day and talked to voters about wages and health care.

Judy Smith's right: this stuff isn't rocket science. Grassroots organizers of every stripe know what grassroots activists do. It's just very rarely written down. Liberal researchers pay close attention to the Right; they often draw complex, spidery maps plotting the political, financial, and social networks that have made it possible for the Right to grow. But when they consider Democrats and their allies, liberal media tend to see only the men at the top and not the relationships.

Maybe Schweitzer tossed somebody's questionnaire in the trash, but he responded to the questionnaire from every "interest" group I've mentioned. Not only did he respond to Montana Conservation Voters' questions, he met with them, both before and after the election, and accepted the endorsement of their PAC, along with the endorsement of the state AFL-CIO, the teachers' unions, and other public interest groups.

When I met with Schweitzer at his home in March 2006, he knew the numbers on the women's vote precisely: "Montana Women Vote registered some seven thousand women to vote, many single women, and they probably voted 80/20 Democrat. There is another four or five thousand into the Democrat camp," he said. "That's important." Brad Martin of the Montana Democrats told reporters after the election, "We reached out early to the prochoice community, the hunting and fishing community, and the folks from the labor movement, and we said, 'Look, you've got to be part of this.'" After his election Schweitzer paid back, creating a new position in his cabinet, an Indian affairs coordinator, and appointing women into top posts.

According to the same conventional wisdom that focuses only on the top of the ticket, the candidate in the biggest race is believed to pull the others along in his or her wake. But take a closer look at who "led" whom to victory in Montana, and it's not so clear who carried what. If anything, the results indicate a bottom-up or reverse-coattails effect. Brian Schweitzer won with just over 50 percent of the vote in a four-way race where his closest competitor, Montana secretary of state Bob Brown, won 46 percent. Schweitzer won in 17 out of 56 counties, in traditional Democratic counties and on the Native American reservations. He did well, but not as well as the other Democratic statewide candidates. (A progressive supreme court justice, Jim Nelson, won with increased support and a bigger margin than Schweitzer's.)

Caferro says she didn't feel any slip-stream spillover of support from Schweitzer as she knocked on her constituents' doors in Helena. Her voters were seeing Schweitzer on TV; they were talking with her face-to-face in their kitchens. In Helena's districts 80 and 81, both Kaufmann and Caferro won with more votes—and a bigger margin of victory—than the governor. Schweitzer won 65 and 54 percent compared to Kaufmann and Caferro's 71 and 58 percent in those districts. "I think there was more of an up-ticket effect," Caferro chuckles. The 2005 session increased the minimum wage for state workers. Caferro carried successful legislation to expand the state's child health care program to cover five thousand more low-income children, and she supported the establishment of a prescription drug assistance program and the elimination of a business tax on small businesses. Kaufmann chaired the Health and Human Services Subcommittee of the House Appropriations Committee. In January 2006 Schweitzer appointed Kaufmann to chair a newly established seven-member advisory council on civil rights. (Dorothy Eck was also appointed to the council.) The two women ran again in 2006, Kaufmann for her fourth term.

For all the fascination with Schweitzer's every move and mannerism, Democrats have paid remarkably little attention to all the various elements that might go into being "Schweitzer-like." One tricky thing for Democrats wishing to seize on the Montana model for Democrats everywhere: Schweitzer goes out of his way to play down that he is a Democrat. Interviewed at his ranch house, his cowboy boots dug deep into the white pile carpet, Brian Schweitzer attributed his success to looking like a Republican. "I'm a third-generation rancher. Nancy and I have been in agribusiness for thirty years. Boy, that sounds just like a Republican," the governor told me, smiling. In 2004 he picked a Republican running mate. One TV ad featured the candidates running for lieutenant governor and governor: "I'm John Bohlinger, I'm a Republican businessman from Billings. And I'm Brian Schweitzer, a Democratic farmer from Whitefish."

Campaigning with U.S. Senate candidate Jon Tester in 2006, not once in half a dozen TV ads was the tag "Democrat" attached to either the governor's or Tester's name. But playing down the Democratic label is not necessarily synonymous with jagging to the right. The establishment media tend to emphasize Schweitzer's break with the party over social issues—he's prochoice but he's also a defender of the right to own guns (no big deal, frankly, out here). His biggest and probably most significant break with the party leadership isn't over any of those things, it's over trade.

In his first race for office in 2000, against incumbent senator Republican Conrad Burns, Schweitzer, following the example of Vermont independent socialist congressman Bernie Sanders, took a group of Montana seniors on a prescription drug–buying trip to Canada, then campaigned against congressional collusion with the drug companies.

Schweitzer opposed NAFTA and took his message directly to Montana family farmers, who'd been feeling the brunt of not-so-free, actually "corporatized" trade. While every Democratic presidential nominee since Bill Clinton has defended the party's support for NAFTA, Schweitzer broke with the pack in 2000 and again in 2004. On the campaign trail in both years, he made trade a top priority. In 2004 he said, "I was a critic of NAFTA. I was a critic of CAFTA [the Central America Free Trade Agreement]. And I'll be a critic of SHAFTA." He drew accolades for his homespun turn of phrase. But it wasn't his sound bite—it was what he had to say that impressed farmers and ranchers in Montana, like family farm activist Helen Waller. Under the rules of the World Trade Organization, trade has been regulated to benefit the biggest producers over the smallest, so farmers like Waller can barely recoup the cost of production from the low prices at which their products sell. A rancher-turned-mint-farmer, Schweitzer talked on the campaign trail about the day the buyer from Crest informed him that he'd be paying ten dollars per pound less for his mint thenceforth because Wal-Mart, which sells half the Crest toothpaste that's sold in this country, had threatened to replace the product with a cheaper Korean brand.

Waller and her colleagues in the Northern Plains Resource Council (an MCV member) were impressed not by Schweitzer's Dean-on-a-ranch swagger but by what he had to say, and those who weren't impressed were at least struck by the fact that he was talking to their issues, Waller tells me. "It's hard in eastern Montana, where people live far apart, to get farmers out to meetings," she says, "especially now that on the national level no one takes any kind of interest." But Schweitzer could attract a crowd. "He'd draw a crowd bigger than any crowd I've ever seen turn out for any politician," Waller reports.

In his first year in office, Schweitzer got points from Waller by supporting renewable energy, wind turbines, and biodiesel fuel. Biodiesel's a product that media pundits tend to poke fun at, but family farmers, increasingly, don't. "Not only do we like the idea of producing an additional crop [oilseed] that we can market, but we use a tremendous amount of diesel fuel to farm," says Waller, who took her first delivery of biodiesel in early 2006. "All around us they are building biodiesel plants as quickly as they can construct them." Promising to invest in biodiesel and wind power, and simply talking to farmers about farmers' issues, Schweitzer went where national Democrats did not, and he came out better for it.

As they headed into the 2006 midterms, however, Waller was less pleased than CBS's Lesley Stahl about the governor's embrace of one nonrenewable energy program, liquid coal. Schweitzer wowed Stahl on national TV with his vial of clear liquid fuel. "It doesn't smell," effused Stahl. To Waller, Schweitzer's liquid fuel program has everything to do with reaching out to Montana's mining industry and nothing to do with preserving clean air. (The process still requires burning coal.)

What passes for mainstream media today makes the unfortunate assumption that trends move like time zones. Dawn breaks over the east and travels west, and change supposedly happens that way too. But a place on the frontier can also be a cutting edge. Montana could offer a window on where the Democratic Party might be headed next. For establishment Democrats, it's likely to be a disconcerting sight.

On the day of the Mansfield-Metcalf Dinner in March 2006, Christine Kaufmann's face, not Schweitzer's, was on the cover of the Helena newspaper. Kaufmann had been pushing the state board of education to draw up an antibullying curriculum that encompassed teaching on racism and homophobia. The Right was up in arms, but it had been maneuvered into a spot where protesting "gay rights" made it appear pro-bully. The curriculum was adopted.

Now the governor is under pressure from Kaufmann to support an LGBT nondiscrimination clause she's proposed to add to Montana's civil rights protections. Helen Waller and Theresa Keaveny are on his case to drop anything having to do with burning coal. "The governor has been great on most of our issues, but we'd like to see him pushing biodiesel and renewables with the same vigor he's brought to liquid fuel," Keaveny told me. And Waller wants to see that Montana's biodiesel is produced right here. "We applaud the governor's commitment to biodiesel, but it needs to be locally produced by Montana farmers," she explained.

In his book *What's the Matter with Kansas?*, Thomas Frank describes how Republican power grew from below. The lesson from Montana is that progressive power grows the same way, first by standing up and then by building support. The question facing Montanans now is which way things will go from here. Some, like Dorothy Eck, are pleased to see a revival of popular participation of the sort that brought citizen constitution-writers to Helena in the winter of 1972. Others, like Senator Max Baucus and some on Schweitzer's staff, appreciate the ground troops that progressives are turning out but not the challenge that primary contenders pose to their party elite.

In Helena these days one sees the national Democratic scenario writ small. Just about everyone's in on the secret that the national media miss: namely, that without progressive movements, there would have been no "Montana miracle." Schweitzer won by just four points; now comes the crunch. The party's mantra is unity, but half the people who've made progress possible are there precisely to stir things up.

In Montana a rabble is rising. Their question is, will they be let into the party structure and shift it, or will they be marginalized and squelched? Unlike those who've been sustained by party machines, those who are coming into office on the backs of independent movements tend to regard commitment to the cause as more important than the maintenance of a united party front. Native American legislators fought so hard for the governor to make good on his promise of substantial new funding for Indian education that the deal had to be worked out in a special session in 2005. "Our numbers certainly added to his win. He knows that, and Indian people know that," says Congresswoman

Carol Juneau. Mary Caferro brought poor mothers into the process; now she wants them to stay. "Everyone knows people will not participate in a system in which they do not see an opportunity to lead," she says. The thrill of being a "ground troop" soon wears off.

In 2006 Montana's profile in Democratic circles kept growing, but style squeezed out substance in most of the reporting, and you can't entirely blame the media for that. Senate candidate Jon Tester's own TV ads talked about Tester's farming, his diet, his crew-cut hair. Most of the rest of the Senate campaign was dedicated to tagging incumbent Burns as a corporate lobbyists' bagman. (No senator received more campaign contributions from crooked lobbyist Jack Abramoff.) In public meetings, Tester spoke out strongly against the Iraq war and the USA Patriot Act. In one debate, when accused of seeking to weaken the act, Tester said he wouldn't just "reform" it; "I'd repeal it." But statements like that didn't get much national play when his victory was finally announced.

Schweitzer stumped for Bill Ritter, elected governor of Colorado, and all over Montana campaign literature for local candidates bore Schweitzer's face (if not the *D* word, *Democrat*). Shortly before the vote, Schweitzer even made an appearance on Comedy Central's hit *The Colbert Report*. Ritter won and Tester won, in a late result that gave the Democrats Senate control.

With such a glow around Schweitzer (and now Tester) on the national stage, it was easy to overlook what happened closer to home. While some results were being contested as this book first went to press, one thing was clear: in only two states around the country did Democrats lose seats in state legislatures, and Montana was one of them, losing five. If Schweitzer's personal popularity is enough to win the day, one would have expected Democrats as a group to win hands down, but they didn't. Certain candidates did just fine, however, carrying progressive policy agendas backed by good organizing: Native candidates for starters. Ten Native Americans—all Democrats—won election to either the state house or the state senate, the most ever. "It shows the power of the Indian vote in Montana," state senator–elect Carol Juneau told *Indian Country Today*. On Juneau's Blackfeet Reservation, 83 percent voted for Tester, making an impact on a tight race. Betsy Hands won in Missoula, keeping a proenvironment, pro–women's rights seat in safe feminist hands. Democrats became the majority on the Public Service Commission when Ken Toole picked up a deciding seat. "This is very conservative country, and yet it seems a died-in-the-wool progressive can be just as competitive as a middler," said Toole. He has pledged to oppose any new round of deregulation. Christine Kaufmann and Mary Caferro were reelected with healthy majorities. Now Caferro wants universal health care and a raise in minimum wages, and if the governor doesn't put his weight behind her bill on civil rights protections, Kaufmann just might bring a domestic partnership bill up for debate in order to raise the heat a little. (She's also considering running for Toole's old seat on the state senate.) Theresa Keaveny and Montana Conservation Voters canvassed 25,000 voters in the last weeks of the campaign. Of the seventy-five candidates supported by MCV, more than half won, and three knocked out three particularly antienvironmental incumbents (not all of them Republicans). A staff person from Helen Waller's Northern Plains Council won election—he'll be in the legislature to vote for biodiesel over liquid coal.

Montana's lesson for Democrats is that miracles do not come easily, and they're certainly not the work of one man alone. Democrats wanting a miracle better be prepared to reward the miracle-makers—all of them.

CHAPTER FOUR ☆ Democratic Dollars

Well, if I'd been a rich man's son

Pay me my money down

I'd sit on the river and watch 'er run

Pay me my money down

Pay me, pay me, pay me my money down

Pay me or go to jail

Pay me my money down.

—Stevedores' song (traditional)

On November 2, 2004, Jo Ann Bowman went to bed happy. By every standard she'd set, her organization, Oregon Action (OA), had achieved tremendous success. It had met ambitious goals for registering and turning out new and infrequent voters, and it even exceeded every one, turning out some sixty thousand on Election Day. Along the way, OA had developed a cohort of new leaders in Oregon's poor, unemployed, and typically most disenfranchised communities. That election night in Portland, OA threw a party, and the room was full of exactly the people the political system usually leaves out. Most had never voted before; several were former felons who'd spent years believing (incorrectly, in Oregon) that they would never regain the right to vote. None had ever watched election returns before, but all were fired up because they could already see their impact. Across town a new mayor was celebrating too. The pro-gay, propoor, former police chief Tom Potter had scored an upset win in Portland that night, in part thanks to ground troops trained and mar-shaled by grassroots groups like Oregon Action. OA had made the dif-ference. Potter knew it; they knew it. The only thought on Bowman's mind was "Now what? What's next?"

Down the coast and across the country, liberal millionaires and bil-lionaires were having a grim night. The hedge fund king George Soros, who had poured a mountain of money into anti-Bush efforts, was expe-riencing the pinch of a bet gone bad. The conservative *National Review* ran a Photoshopped cover portrait of Soros in a black shirt that read, "I SPENT $27 MILLION AND ALL I GOT WAS THIS LOUSY T-SHIRT!"

Liberal donors hardly needed a catty magazine shot to point out the painfully obvious. Matching the Republicans, whom they love to call big spenders, rich Democrats had maxed out on campaign contri-butions, then dipped into their fortunes and their phone books to give to liberal advocacy groups and get their friends to do the same. While Soros was the top donor, two dozen individuals donated $2 million or more, and a few hundred contributed at least $100,000 each. They had still lost the election. There were no victory parties at the Soroses' on November 2, nor were they celebrating in the San Francisco Bay Area home of the Rappaports in Woodside. Deborah Rappaport and her venture capitalist husband, Andrew, had donated close to $5 million. For them, election night was a punch in the gut. "We couldn't believe it. We went into shock for a bit," she told me.

Different groups measure progress in different ways. The most powerful people in the Democratic camp were devastated by the 2004 outcome; longtime movement activists like Bowman mostly were not. In part that's because the George Soroses of the world tend to measure progress by return on investments and bang for the buck. Jo Ann Bowman measures progress by people like Jerome Akles. A forty-three-year-old nonvoting former felon with a history of drugs and street crime, Akles, at the end of OA's seven-month leadership program, was meeting with politicians, speaking to the media, and mentoring youth. He personally signed up six hundred brand-new voters in 2004, many of them former felons. Unfortunately, as Bowman prepared to take Oregon Action's work to the next level and reach a whole new generation of leaders-in-the-making like Akles, the group's resources shriveled. "It happens every four years," she says resignedly. "We see money come in when people think we're useful. Then when the election's over, it dries up."

The election did not fundamentally change Bowman's plans, but it did change the Democratic donors'. Donors like Rappaport resolved to throw the old ways out and as the Apple ads say, "Think different," to find a new approach. Rappaport says, "We had been good, obedient Democrats for years. We'd done everything the party asked us to do. Then 2002 happened, and then 2004, and we realized what we were doing wasn't working. We've got to do something else."

The 2004 elections were a defeat not only for a candidate, but for a whole Democratic Party way of doing things. The best description for that is "Scrooge democracy." For decades, the Democratic Party establishment has run its national operation like a Dickensian workhouse. Instead of building up state-based infrastructure and relying (as they once did) on influential party bosses, in the late twentieth century, Democratic Party leaders in Washington preferred to talk to voters via direct mail and television, and to keep their base organizations weak, dependent, and politically under D.C.'s control. Come election

season, nonprofit groups and labor unions could be contracted to register voters and get out the vote as needed and do the street-level work.

The 2004 elections did not empower Democrats—they were still
locked out of power in every federal government branch—but the
campaign experience certainly did empower Democratic donors. New
campaign finance laws allowed nonparty groups called 527s to do all
the things a party could do except write a platform and run a candidate
for office. America Coming Together (ACT), America Votes, and the
Campaign for America's Future—all 527s—hired field staff to register
voters and get out the vote; they produced TV ads, conducted polls,
and carried out voter education. Such 527s raised unbelievable amounts
of money, for the first time matching the donors on the Right. (ACT
and the Media Fund, another 527, raised more than $200 million simply
for use in field operations.) They had a tremendous impact in 2004,
turning out more votes in target states than ever before. But the party
itself, and its consultants, suffered defeats. Many donors concluded
that they no longer had any reason to believe that the party knew best.
All at once a class of empowered liberal entrepreneurs was released to
roam free. They were on a mission—and on the lookout for a silver
bullet.

That's the American way, especially if you're affluent. For every
pang there is relief. The promise of a rescue-remedy is as American as
apple pie or as snake oil. In the fall of 2004, prescriptions to remedy the
Democrats' plight were written in rich abundance. One proposal in
particular was primed and ready. The buzz grew about a PowerPoint
presentation titled *The Conservative Message Machine's Money Matrix.*
Suddenly influential people who had just been talking about elections
were chattering instead about a "money matrix." Instead of "get votes,"
the hot words now on wealthy lips were "get infrastructure, get media,
get think tanks."

Ironically, the most popular remedy to cure what ailed the Bad Old

Democrats came from inside the BOD themselves. The *Money Matrix* PowerPoint prescription was the work of Rob Stein, a former chief of staff to Clinton's commerce secretary, and Simon Rosenberg, a former DLC (Democratic Leadership Council) official. After the 2002 elections, Stein reportedly woke up with a start to find that the United States had acquired a one-party government. He set out to discover how the conservative movement had taken control. What he found he condensed onto forty-three color slides that he and Rosenberg took on the road.

The *Money Matrix* presentation laid out the road map of right-wing power, its sources, its structure, its impact. Its narrative was familiar to those who'd researched the Right for years before Stein came along. Boiled down to the basics, the story goes like this: a small consortium of conservative donors and foundations invested huge amounts of money into policy shops and think tanks that used media and lobbying brilliantly to gain influence and power and shove the country to the right. Stein and Rosenberg showed their PowerPoint plan to megadonors George Soros and Peter Lewis and then their networks. The idea caught on that if the "think different" donors could just fund enough think tanks, advocacy groups, and media, they could do for democracy and for Democrats what the Right's patrons had done for Reagan and Bush.

The timing was perfect. Fed up with losing, loyal liberal donors wanted a new plan, and Stein's presentation provided one: learn from the Right, then win. One group of donors became particularly jazzed. "In thirty minutes, Stein's PowerPoint brought the history of the Right together in a way that nobody had seen before," says Guy Saperstein, a retired civil rights attorney and Sierra Club board member. "It's not that there's a lack of funding; there's a lack of strategic funding on the Left," he told me he realized. That lack came as a shock to some people, admitted Saperstein, and those forty-three slides ignited a new funding circle—the Democracy Alliance (DA). The alliance's goal was to help funders on the Left be as strategic as the Right's donors had been, and to educate donors who were not very familiar with politics. As Saperstein admits, individual donors acting solo can be "erratic." "It's not always very rational. Your recipients can be the last person you talked to in an elevator, or the friend of a friend. A lot of philanthropists make a lot of nonstrategic decisions." Alliance staff and partner committees promised to act as a kind of clearinghouse for donors besieged by myriad grant-seekers. In exchange, the donors pledged to give away a million dollars each over three years. At its launch, in August 2005, the alliance comprised eighty "donor partners," all eager to get to work.

Will the Democracy Alliance donors make a difference? Their impact is already being felt. The conversation that Stein sparked afresh has encouraged all sorts of groups to compare the Left's situation with the Right's. And the research they are producing is prodding funders to reassess.

In her brightly lit office at People for the American Way in New York, Iara Peng is the essence of hopeful. Bright and well media-trained, Peng is the director of Young People For, a group she founded with the help of Norman Lear and People for the American Way on the day after Election Day, November 3, 2004. "You voted, now what?" is the group's slogan; its mission is to connect campus activists to one another and to broader progressive movements. When we talk in June 2006, Peng is just back from attending a Democracy Alliance meeting in Austin. Participants were sworn to secrecy, but the scuttlebutt was that Bill Clinton showed up and that Saperstein drove him into a fury by challenging his wife's and his own position on Iraq and U.S. troop withdrawal. A few months before the 2006 elections, the DA partners weren't in any presidential candidate's pocket (yet), but they were thrilled to bits about some of the proposals they'd seen, and thirty-year-old Peng (who mentions her age to ensure I don't take her for younger) must have wowed them.

Peng shows me a set of graphs she's worked up on her computer. The first one plots total grants to nine conservative organizations that target young people, among them the Young Americas Foundation, the Intercollegiate Studies Institute, and the Leadership Institute. The line on Peng's graph slants steadily upward to just under $50 million in total grants from conservative foundations in 2003. The funding to the groups is steady and consistent, growing their median budgets from just over $3 million in 2000 to $3,500,000 in 2003. Then she shows me a graph of the same picture on the progressive side: liberal foundations spend less than a tenth of what their right-wing counterparts do. The graph line is a jagged dragon's tail of funding peaks and valleys, coinciding with election cycles. It's money for getting out votes, not building leaders to head a movement. "How do we expect young people to commit to us if we won't commit to them?" Peng asks. She can list the influential conservatives whom the Right invested in as youths: in 1970 Karl Rove headed up National College Republicans; in 1981 Grover Norquist held that job; in 1983 it was Ralph Reed.

I'm reminded of a charming young man I dined with in Salt Lake City. Zach Howell, chairman of Federation of College Republicans, had just turned twenty, but already he'd been to six free (or almost free) national conferences attended by fellow student conservatives and addressed by a pantheon of right-wing luminaries. He'd heard Pat Buchanan, Newt Gingrich, Tom DeLay, Paul Weyrich—he rattled off the names as other kids would recite their baseball card collection. He felt sorry for his school's College Democrats. "We get a welcome box every semester from the RNC, full of free stuff for new recruits and free magazines and training materials. They've sent it for years." Even though his campus is overwhelmingly Democratic, College Dems received their first care package from the DNC only in 2005. Said Howell: "I feel bad for them."

Among those who follow the funding world, whatever their opinion of Stein or initiatives like the Democracy Alliance may be, the most commonly heard response is relief that at least the subject of infrastructure is coming in for some new attention. John Cavanagh at the Institute for Policy Studies, a left-wing think tank in Washington, D.C., echoed a commonly held view when he told me, "Three years ago you didn't even have a conversation about the need to think long term or build progressive infrastructure. At least now that conversation's happening."

Up to now activism in the electoral arena has been hampered by the fact that even those few foundations that are dedicated to changing U.S. government policy are regulated by the government. Organizations— including foundations—can't generally receive donations or government grants unless they have nonprofit status, most commonly 501c(3). In exchange for what amounts to a public subsidy from the government, nonprofits are required to abide by certain rules—have corporate-style boards, maintain open records, hold public meetings—and they're not supposed to engage in partisan politics. Right-wing activists in the 1960s seized on a certain public discomfort with public sponsorship of some activist work (nonprofits working with peace groups, say, or civil rights activists). Conservatives dragged the directors of Ford and Rockefeller and Carnegie into Congress in the 1960s to defend themselves from allegations of partisanship.

In reality, nonprofit groups are permitted to organize, speak on issues, and even lobby, so long as lobbying doesn't consume a significant share of their activities. (Another classification that groups can apply for—501c(4) status—permits unlimited lobbying, but the donors don't get tax breaks.) Focus on the Family, the largest Religious Right organization in the world, with a budget in excess of $128 million, allots about a tenth of its expenses for lobbying activities, as identified on its

2005 tax return. Focus has a staff of thirteen hundred employees to de-code the rulebooks if the IRS challenges its filing. Among liberal foundations and the groups they fund, on the other hand, fear of an audit and loss of status (or humiliation in Congress) runs rampant.

Well-organized entrepreneurs, like those in the Democracy Alliance, have the money to go where foundations won't, affording themselves the freedom that a skittish board of directors lacks. Democracy Alliance is a 501c(4), not a c(3). Its partners are firm that they are not forming a foundation.

Deborah Rappaport has a very clear idea of the kind of work she wants to fund. With a few exceptions Rappaport says she's temporarily swearing off campaign contributions: "I can't support the party leadership at this point until they take a stronger position on Iraq." What she wants to fund now is small, new, and grassroots. In 2005 she started the New Progressive Coalition (NPC), a website that operates a kind of online dating service for progressive philanthropists seeking mates for their money and skills. "Investors" peruse proposals online, and for a sliding-scale fee (starting at $100) the NPC makes tax lawyers, accountants, and other professionals available to grant-seekers free or at a massively cut rate.

Liberated donors like these have the power to give the Bad Old Democrats one hell of a headache. In the run-up to the 2006 midterms, the Democrats' congressional and senatorial campaign committee chairs were facing an uphill, off-year fund-raising battle, and donors striking out on their own didn't help. Rappaport's attitude is one I heard a lot. Having given to the party for years, she's now prioritizing her giving someplace else—in her case, state-based organizing projects. She hopes to fund programs in ten or eleven swingable states before 2008. "Movement is more difficult to fund than get-out-the-vote, where you can count the votes," she says. But she hopes to instill in progressive groups some business sense. Demanding that groups set goals, find ways of measuring their impact, and regularly review their own work is Rappaport's way of instilling some system of analysis, or metrics, into a typically rather scattershot world. "Part of what we're doing is bringing the lessons of the business world into the nonprofit and political world. Many of the values are the same; the skill set isn't," she tells me. For their own personal giving, the Rappaports have set up a foundation, Skyline Public Works, that specializes in supporting youth and start-ups. "We like to be in first."

The good news is that a lot of potentially powerful people are talk-ing about "infrastructure" and "movement." The bad news is, they're not actually movement folks. When I ask Rappaport how she's going to locate the close-to-the-ground authentic leaders in North Carolina, say, where she wants to sponsor a project, she says she'll ask former sen-ator and vice-presidential candidate John Edwards. Rappaport, mother of three and a local school board trustee, has never been this involved in politics; her only previous link to professional politics had been hosting parties for candidates. Lacking a background in organizing, but possessed of a sense of purpose, she is part of a generation that believes anything is possible if you pull together enough money and expertise and passion. That's certainly proven to be true in her husband's career. She grew up in the 1960s, when movements really did overhaul the na-tion's laws and culture; whether it's true or not, baby boomers tend to believe they were personally part of that overhaul.

In their rush to have an impact, some fear new, entrepreneurial funders may overlook the old in favor of the new, on the assumption that what's already been around for a while must not be working. As Guy Saperstein admits, Democracy Alliance meetings operate more or less like auction houses (my word, not his). Selected grant-seekers make their presentation to the group; then donors write checks. "There's an element of checkbook democracy to the process," he says. "What excites people the most are the newer, more energized groups."

John Cavanagh at the Institute for Policy Studies (IPS) is understandably concerned about the funding trend toward the new. At forty years old, IPS is one of the oldest think tanks on the Left. What's needed may be more money for networking and coordination, rather than new creations built from scratch, says Cavanagh, who wonders if progressive funders even know what the liberal-to-left universe looks like. "If you name a hundred and fifty organizations on the Right, you've pretty much named most of them. On our side, a real map would have tens of thousands of groups, but they're not linked into national structures, like parties; they're all over the place, uncoordinated." He's got a point. The twentieth-century Democratic base had its roots in black churches and blue-collar union halls, and those are still the structures on which the party groups rely, but look at who actually mobilizes every election today, and you'll find a world of institutions that expands way beyond blue and black. Workers' centers, gay community centers, women's health clinics, art galleries, theaters, and independent book shops: liberals and the Left have a universe of institutions that has yet to be tracked, let alone adequately funded and built into networks. Liberals have become good at mapping the Right; what's needed is a nifty PowerPoint presentation on the Left.

If you wanted to map what already exists on the progressive spectrum, Oregon's not a bad place to start. Since November 2004, even without big-donor assistance, Oregon Action has grown its base, drawn more members into the political system, and had a direct impact on goings-on in its home state. On May 18, 2005, the Portland, Oregon, city council voted four to one to approve voter-owned elections for city officials, making it the first city in the country to adopt full public financing along the lines of the systems in place in Arizona, North Carolina, and Maine. Under the new Portland law, candidates have to collect five-dollar qualifying contributions (1,000 for auditor and city council, 1,500 for mayor), reject private donations, and limit campaign spending. In return, they receive a capped amount of campaign dollars from a publicly financed fund. Almost as soon as Mayor Potter signed the new law, lobbyists for the utility companies and other big businesses began gathering signatures to put a repeal initiative on the ballot. Their effort failed, but the lobbyists didn't give up. Next in their sights were the commissioners who had passed the new law—most notably, Erik Sten, the law's author. Sten was running for reelection in the first cohort of publicly financed candidates. As corporate contributions flooded to Sten's opponent, Oregon Action's Jo Ann Bowman geared up to get her group to act. Oregon Action is a poor-people's organization, not an election reform outfit, and campaign financing is hardly the juiciest subject in the beauty parlor or the supermarket. Bowman says she knew it was going to take some work to stir her members. The person she turned to wasn't an expert from a think tank, it was Jerome Akles. Akles knows how to convey a passionate message about people having a voice in elections because he himself feels it. He thought he'd lost his voice when he went to prison, and he's not about to have it drowned out now by some money-bags lobbyist. Oregon Action's members collected five-dollar bills from people who'd never in their lives imagined becoming campaign contributors. With the group's help, Sten won his race against several candidates who had been backed by business. It made his contributors proud. "Voter-owned elections create a system in which politicians are accountable to us, not big-money campaign donors," says Bowman.

"You want different framing—put different people in the frame," says Dan Petegorsky of the Portland-based Western States Center. The center, founded in 1987, works with statewide progressive coalitions in Utah, Wyoming, Nevada, and Idaho. The weekend I'm in town, the board of directors is meeting, comprising representatives from the Progressive Leadership Alliance in Nevada, the Idaho Women's Network,

United Vision for Idaho, the Equality State Policy Center (Wyoming), and the Utah Progressive Network. Talking with the members, I'm struck by how, working regionally, activists get smarter more quickly. Western States isn't called a think tank, but it should be. In the late 1980s and 1990s, when no one in Washington was focusing on the Northwest, Petegorsky and his colleagues were analyzing how antienvironmentalist Wise Use groups and the Religious Right were tapping into local grievances and turning the region into an around-the-clock testing ground for right-wing ballot initiatives.

Basic Rights Oregon didn't need a business plan to force it to change its tactics; in 2004 change was forced on it by events. A lesbian, gay, bisexual, and transgendered justice group in Portland, Basic Rights had been doing the same thing for more than a decade, fighting right-wing ballot initiatives. Since 1988 conservative backlash groups have advanced literally scores of initiatives that have attempted to do everything from restricting abortion access to banning gay employment in schools and same-sex marriage. Since 1992 every measure had been defeated, but the Right's signature gatherers keep coming back, and in 2004 they finally won a majority—58 percent of Oregon voters approved measure 36, an amendment to the state constitution that bans marriage between people of the same sex.

"With so much practice, we were great at responding to crisis; what we had to figure out was how to mount an offense," Roey Thorpe, director of Basic Rights Oregon, told me. Consulting with allies in the state senate and movement lawyers, the group helped legislators write a civil unions bill that was introduced in the 2005 legislative session. Basic Rights Oregon organized more than one thousand people to come out to lobby. "For once we were working *for* something, not against." First time out, Senate Bill 1000 passed two to one, only to be denied a hearing in the house. Every major newspaper in the state supported the proposal, which Thorpe is sure is a safe bet to pass when it finally gets a vote.

Oregon was one of the first states in the nation to experience the Right's onslaught on gay issues. Over the years Thorpe's group has built relationships with a spectrum of allies, from NARAL Pro-Choice America, the SEIU, and the Oregon Rural Organizing Project to Pineros y Campesinos Unidos del Noroeste, the local farmworkers and tree planters group. "We've been successful in changing the debate and putting a new face on our movement," says Roey. She says she'd like to share what she's learned with others but she barely has a travel budget. The National Gay and Lesbian Task Force has an annual organizing conference every year called Creating Change. According to activists, the workshops there are invaluable. But from year to year, that's about all there is.

In over a decade, while it was busy defeating cutting-edge right-wing initiatives, Basic Rights Oregon never received a multiyear grant. "Even our friends make us apply every year," Thorpe says frostily, and local groups must compete for grants not only with one another but with national organizations. "I guess local's not sexy enough," quips Thorpe. Today's entrepreneur-minded funders talk about "metrics" and demonstrable outcomes. Thorpe looks at a record of success that has made Oregon a model for organizers nationwide and wonders how much better could they do: "What metrics are they thinking of?"

Thorpe's not alone asking that question. Right next door, in special elections in November 2005, Californians rejected six right-wing legislative initiatives that dealt with access to abortion, authority over union dues, and lobbying. It was an utter defeat for the Terminator himself: California governor Arnold Schwarzenegger had personally endorsed four of the measures. But it was a triumph for coalitions of community-based progressive groups that have been organizing aggressively for years—the same groups that paved the way for the former union leader and ACLU board member Democrat Antonio Villaraigosa to become mayor of Los Angeles in May 2005.

If liberal funders spent half the time studying the successes of the Left that they spend obsessing over the Coors foundation, they'd be better informed, not to mention cheerier. Funders searching for a model of successful infrastructure-building by a foundation would be hard pressed to find a better example than the slow and steady grants program of the Liberty Hill Foundation in Los Angeles. Liberty Hill has modest assets (around $6 million in 2003, just under that in 2004); it distributed about the same amount in grants that year. The foundation is part of a network of donor-advised community funds that, were they on the right, we'd call a "cabal," coordinated by the New York–based National Funding Exchange. Torie Osborn, a feminist with a history of work in NOW and in the AIDS and LGBT movements, served as Liberty Hill's director for most of the past decade. She recalls that in the early 1990s Liberty Hill convened a kind of activists' brain trust to take stock. The uprisings that set South Central L.A. on fire in 1992 pushed that brain trust into high gear. Drawing on their local advisers' expertise, the foundation (and others like it, including Colin Greer's New World Foundation) began giving small seed grants to community organizations, offering technical assistance, and yes, caring.

Activists who'd come up in the Black Power, Chicano, Asian, Asian Pacific Islander, and United Farm Workers movements realized they needed to come together to build local leadership in politically and economically abandoned communities. When grant-makers talk about long-term funding, they usually mean three years. In L.A. it took ten: grass roots grow slowly. But the information and experience that organizers gather along the way can be put to many purposes. Anthony Thigpenn and Adrianne Shropshire at L.A.'s SCOPE/AGENDA (a Liberty Hill and New World grantee) mapped the area and figured out where the leaders were located, what power lay where, and where new groups needed to start. After a decade Liberty Hill's grassroots projects had built a coalition that, while nonpartisan, had enough local leadership and mobilizing capacity to turn out voters and affect elections, even to elect their own. Karen Bass, a former Black Panther who founded the Community Coalition in L.A. in 1990, ran for office and was elected to the state assembly in 2004. Villaraigosa (who joined the advisory board of the Liberty Hill Foundation in 1996) was elected mayor in January 2005. The massive immigration marches that took most observers aback later that year were no surprise to the Liberty Hill staff. "Liberty Hill has invested $4.5 million in immigrant rights work in L.A. since 2000," communications director Barbara Osborn told *In These Times* in July 2006. "What erupted on the streets March 25 was no accident and no surprise to us." All those immigrant marches in heartland states? Funding Exchange members have been funding comparable immigrant rights groups around the country for years.

You'd think funders would be throwing money at the groups that mobilized downtrodden Angelinos to elect a mayor and that helped stop the Terminator in his tracks, but no. Adrianne Shropshire says that Los Angeles groups, which by 2005 had built a statewide coalition called the California Alliance, expected to see an influx of money, but it didn't happen. The California Alliance has since linked up with sister groups in Mississippi, Kentucky, Alabama, New Mexico, and New York to go after national grant money as a united front. Calling themselves the PushBack Alliance, the statewide partners have long track records and proven potential and ability to collaborate. They *are* progressive infrastructure, but so far, apparently, not the sort the "think different" funders like. At the Democracy Alliance, for example, at least in year one, they didn't make it out of the committee process.

Adrianne Shropshire is hopeful that things are changing, "but when it comes to new think tanks and new messaging machines, the money still isn't out there for field organizing." "Field" gets a bad rap in general, says Shropshire, who directed field operations for the California Alliance and now heads up Jobs with Justice in New York. Another question gets to the heart of the matter: Who are funders comfortable investing in, in the field? . . . "There's a pretty offensive dismissal of community-based groups, even those with a track record of getting the job done," she says. We're talking, of course, about people-of-color-led groups. According to a 2005 report by the Greenlining Institute, independent foundations award only 3 percent of all grant dollars, and 4.3 percent of grants go to people-of-color-led organizations. Five foundations in the research sample awarded no grants to people-of-color-led organizations at all. The supposedly liberal community foundations awarded only 3 percent of grant dollars and 2 percent of grants to so-called minority-led groups. In Los Angeles, and probably in California as a whole (if the census is accurate), and shortly to be true in many states, people of color aren't minorities—they're in the majority. They're a Democratic majority too—in fact, they're *the* Democratic majority—the only demographic group (except for young voters) that consistently votes blue by large margins. If Democrats (big and also little *d*) don't care about majorities, what do they care about? In its first year the Democracy Alliance funded just one people-of-color-led organization, ACORN. The Alliance is 95 percent white (and about 60 percent male). That's inevitable, I'm told, given who has dispensable wealth in this country. But one philanthropist approached by the Alliance had an easy solution to the "inevitability" of whiteness. She agreed to pledge her $1 million over the years on condition that a black Baptist minister organizer whom she admired could participate in alliance meetings in her stead. She was turned down flat.

Seeking to fight the Right, today's liberal donors say they want a new approach, but for expertise they seem to be turning to the same old experts, including Rob Stein, a graduate of the Clinton administration, who by his own account woke up to the Right's advance only a few years back. Perhaps it's because in the 1980s and 1990s, most of today's new donors were not much involved in politics. As megadonor Rob Glaser, CEO of the software company Real Networks (and a major investor in Air America Radio), put it candidly to me, "Most of us spent the eighties and nineties pretty much getting rich." A lot of others, meanwhile, were getting to know the conservative movement well, from close up, as its targets. A few of those people are now in a position to put their expertise to use, having risen to leadership in some well-endowed foundations.

If you looking for a liberal Karl Rove or Paul Weyrich, Rodger McFarlane just might be that person. In March 2004 McFarlane became the executive director of the Denver-based Gill Foundation, founded by Quark software entrepreneur Tim Gill after his state passed an anti–gay marriage constitutional amendment (later overturned by the Supreme Court) in 1994. Gill himself is a major campaign contributor, one of the top six individual givers to 527 groups in 2006. His nonprofit foundation funds anti-AIDS and LGBT groups through the Gill Action Fund, the foundation's affiliated 501c(4). McFarlane brought to the job years of experience in activism: having helped found ACT UP (the AIDS Coalition to Unleash Power) and having served as director of the Gay Men's Health Crisis, the first—and in its heyday, the largest—volunteer AIDS organization in the United States and the world. As a gay man, McFarlane told me, he started researching the organized Right in the late 1970s as he watched the antigay movement advance. Now in a position to put what he's learned from the Right into effect on his own movement's behalf, he's been at Gill funding in-depth opinion research on gay issues and pulling LGBT funders together to draw up a long-term plan to achieve gay equality. Among those he's convening are several who also came up through anti-AIDS and LGBT activism, and now direct family foundations with significant funds. Once grantees, now they're grantors, and they're doing their best to model new donor strategies. In 2005 the Michigan-based Arcus Foundation, directed by Urvashi Vaid, announced a $3 million grant to the National Gay and Lesbian Task Force (years ago directed by Vaid), the biggest single gift to any LGBT group. Other funders are building what they call the Equality Federation, a new coalition of state groups that intends to help local activists connect and share tactics. By the year 2020 (give or take five years), says McFarlane, the goal is for ten states to have full-marriage equality; ten more to have civil unions or the equivalent; ten to have nondiscrimination laws and to be repealing (or peeling back the effects of) their anti–gay marriage amendments; and the final twenty states to show progress.

McFarlane's work is being felt outside the LGBT arena as well. Democrats reeled out of 2004 with just two state-level success stories: Montana and Colorado. In Colorado, a state that voted 52 to 47 percent for Bush over Kerry, Democrats won control over both houses of the state legislature and picked up one of just two Democratic gains in the U.S. Senate. Backstage at the GOP's debacle were four determined and creative funders, one of whom was Tim Gill, who is advised by McFarlane and political adviser Ted Trimpa. With three other major donors—Pat Stryker, Jared Polis, and Rutt Bridges—Gill poured a combined $1.6 million into an election operation in Colorado that did what the Democrats so far hadn't done—namely, win. The "four horsemen," as they came to be called, marshaled local progressive groups into a voter-registration and get-out-the-vote army, and they paid for withering ads against their least-favorite incumbents, transforming what could have been no-contest races into big-money-sucking fights for the Right. A 37-to-28 GOP advantage in the statehouse flipped over into a 35-to-30 Democratic edge. Democrats picked up a state senate seat to switch the balance in that branch from 18 to 17 Republican to 19 to 17 Democratic, and Ken Salazar won his Senate race 51 to 47 percent.

McFarlane and Gill are nowhere near finished. A software engineer, Tim Gill is no ideologue. "He's barely even a Democrat," says McFarlane. But he's fed up with the right-wing wrecking ball that's been swinging at the lives of gay men like himself. He wants to win, and he's willing to pay for it. And he has no board or membership to hold him back. In the 2004 general election, Gill was up there with George Soros among the top-ten individual givers in the United States. Imagine Donald Trump had a gay brother dead-set on building not casinos and condominiums, but effective fight-back power in all fifty states. At six foot six, McFarlane has no time for bullies. Foul-mouthed, flamboyant, and as cutthroat as the Broadway producer he once was, McFarlane honeycoats his gruffness with a treacly Texas accent, but the passion is clear: as happened in the AIDS crisis, "Nothing will make me stay up all night and work harder than [seeing a bully pick] on somebody weaker than you. Then I get really righteous and competitive and ugly, and I'm a big mean guy, and so is my boss, and he is richer than shit."

McFarlane has about as much patience for campaigns that try hard but lose as Donald Trump has for feeble apprentices. "Tim doesn't pay me to try really hard," McFarlane barks. For the last few years Gill's been funding Melanie Sloan, the genius prosecutor behind the Committee to Restore Ethics in Washington, the group that took down GOP House majority leader Tom DeLay by investigating his campaign practices and turning a spotlight on GOP corruption. Sloan has more targets in her political crosshairs, and McFarlane's backing her with more of Tim Gill's cash. "When she takes out two more, then I'll go back to Tim for more money," he says.

A former lover of the playwright Larry Kramer, McFarlane sees politics as a production in which the politicians have to believe they're leading men but are actually bit players. They have to please and strut their stuff, but the production's backed by investors they've never met. "We shape what show they're in, what script they're reading, and when and how they read it," says McFarlane. "And it's our investors who are determining what show goes up."

As he tells it, McFarlane raised millions of dollars from gay businessmen for Bill Clinton in 1992, and in exchange the LGBT community got don't-ask-don't-tell and Clinton's signature on the Right's Defense of Marriage Act. "Politicians will say whatever they have to say to get power and to exercise power. So I either have to make [them] more successful or punish [them] bitterly when [they sell] me out. . . . We have to hurt them. And we never hurt Bill Clinton." Today Gill and his colleagues write $3 million checks without sweating over a tax deduction. "My seven donors together represent a very large percentage of the soft money on the Democratic side," McFarlane told me in early 2006. "They don't give it to the party anymore. They make their own deals with candidates state by state."

It's not the most democratic way to make change, but so far McFarlane's approach comes closer than the Democracy Alliance has to matching the Right, plan for plan, attack with attack. Like Adolph Coors, McFarlane knows what he wants. The same cannot be said for the DA crowd. They're good folks, but one has a devilish time nailing them down on their goals. It's not just their cloak-and-dagger approach to secrecy; either they don't know or they're scared of saying what they want. Guy Saperstein has taken on the task of convening a subcommittee on strategy. "It's something the Alliance is grappling with. I've had people say 'Don't seek an overarching strategy because when you do that, some people won't agree.'"

If you don't declare a destination, it's hard-to-impossible to settle on a route. Most DA donors, if they were to be brutally honest, would admit that they want to elect Democrats. So be it—it's quite possibly the thing they do best. In 2006 George Soros spent another $1.6 million on

America Votes, which was passed on to America Coming Together. His colleague Peter Lewis gave just a shade under $1 million to America Votes and in personal contributions. The Rappaports kept to their word, mostly giving money to progressive start-ups and nothing to the Democratic Senatorial Campaign Committee. Those with individual power, like Tim Gill, to write big checks without oversight or accountability (except to the FEC) could match the Right's Olin, Scaife, and Bradley, if they built power methodically in the states. The Right's dominance was built incrementally, statehouse by statehouse, attorney general by attorney general, judicial bench by bench. Laying the groundwork for the Reagan "revolution" took more than a decade. "The dominance since then has been pretty systematic. I'd argue it's not been grassroots," says McFarlane. "It's been like every government in history—it's a class elite that's behind it."

Jean Hardisty, who has been studying right-wing political movements since the 1970s, is glad to see donors sitting down to study their giving habits, but part of her, she admits, would like to say "Stop—don't give a dime" until you've spent years learning. As she has said for years, building a movement is different from supporting a candidate for office. The winning takes longer, and the losses are great. Meanwhile, Hardisty adds, "There's this illusion that the Right goes crashing into communities and throws out money to manipulate and control people. Actually, that's a good description of what progressives do."

The fact is, ideas are like songs. Stein's *Money Matrix* presentation came along at the right time, in the right package, with the right credentials, but it was a cover version of an analysis that opposition researchers and a few journalists had been laying out for years. In 1981 Jean Hardisty founded Political Research Associates to monitor the advance of the Right. She and her colleague Chip Berlet and writers Sara Diamond, Frederick Clarkson, Russ Bellant, Suzanne Pharr, Tarso Ramos, and Lee Cokorinos have plotted the growth of the right wing for decades, their work appearing in low-budget journals like PRA's *Public Eye* and magazines like *In These Times, The Progressive, Color Lines, The Nation,* and *Ms.*

"The political Right currently runs the country. That's very annoying," Chip Berlet wrote in 2005. "What is really annoying is that in the late 1970s some of us were giving speeches and writing articles explaining that rightists intended to take over the country. It wasn't hard to figure that out, since at the same time ideologues and strategists were also giving speeches and writing articles describing in elaborate detail how they planned to do it. Well, they did it."[1] With so much experience researching the Right, and more spent observing and consulting groups on the Left, Hardisty believes that liberals don't understand some things about the Right, and that some aspects of the typical *Matrix* narrative just aren't accurate.

For one thing, the image of a "single-minded cabal" is misleading. In an essay co-written with Deepak Bhargava for *The Nation,* Hardisty said that there is no single conservative movement but rather a plethora of ideologies harnessed together in coalition. The groups didn't all agree, "but they started out with inquiry into core beliefs." Some of those began far outside the mainstream of opinion but have since migrated to the middle of society, expressed as support for "family values," "limited government," and "military dominance."

Another missed lesson from the Right, says Hardisty, is the value of listening: "No one ever handed down a think-tanked message that sparked a movement." The Right forged new alliances by going to those who had grievances. In the early 1970s Kevin Phillips, a former Nixon speechwriter, picked up on rising rage in his New York neighborhood. "Educators, consultants and media executives [have replaced] yesteryear's population of bankers, railroad vice-presidents and merchants" as targets of popular resentment, Phillips wrote in 1975. The Right then came out swinging against professors and the press—

what Phillips called "the multibillion-dollar social engineering industry." Leaders of the *National Review* and the Conservative Caucus once visited laid-off steelworkers in Ohio and returned ecstatic about just how angry workers were—not at their bosses, but at the federal government. Soon thereafter, Richard Viguerie announced a massive direct-mail campaign to union members.

Conservative groups have learned how to adapt so as to make hay of resentments and channel them to build their movements. Today's liberals are always calling for those with grievances to put them aside and sign on with the party agenda as it has been fixed. That approach ignores the power of social movements, which historically have pulled politicians toward them, not the reverse. "Think tanks and their output of ideas . . . are a necessary but not sufficient component of any social movement," wrote Hardisty and Bhargava. Trade unions are mass-membership organizations, with independent income coming from member dues. While unions are disparaged by liberal pundits and discouraged by the policies of centrist Democrats, the Right's mass-membership groups, like the National Rifle Association, the Moral Majority, and Focus on the Family have grown in power in the lobbying halls of Congress and in the streets. Membership groups serve their members, not far-off donors. At a Focus on the Family church you can bring your kid in on his birthday, and he'll get a cake. "There's a room all ready in the back with balloons and bunting and you can throw a party for your kid and his friends right there. What harried parent wouldn't love that?" Hardisty asked me over tea in New York. "Service your members. Caring. We don't do it."

The other problem with the centralization of power in liberal donors' hands arises when the donors' interests and those of progressive America conflict. When the Seattle fair trade movement brought hundreds of thousands into the streets in the early 2000s, and demanded a fundamental change in the Democratic Party's approach to business, international trade, and economic development, its demands went smack up against not the evil Right but the Democratic establishment and its biggest corporate funders, who applauded Bill Clinton's signature on the centerpiece of so-called free trade policy—NAFTA.

The biggest new funder on the block, the Democracy Alliance, has raised a lot of expectations, and many progressive groups have dedicated countless hours to preparing proposals for the alliance, hours that could have been spent on other work instead. Most have been disappointed. There is always in the world of funding what Jon Sinton, one of the founders of Air America Radio, calls the possibility of "death by a thousand positive meetings." More worrying, some groups report (anonymously) that their own donors have decreased their giving, in order to channel it through the Alliance instead. At the end of 2006, Political Research Associates was facing a major reduction in funds from the Ford Foundation, and the economic fight of its life. Has PRA received any money from the Democracy Alliance, I asked Chip Berlet. He answered strategically. "No, not yet."

What does hold potential is the donors' demand that grant recipients develop income streams and become self-sufficient. Barbara Dudley, former director of the Veatch Foundation (a donor-advised fund based in the Unitarian Universalist Church) and former director of Greenpeace (the environmentalist organization), believes it's time for progressive movement groups to get out of "sandbox politics." Underfunded and dependent on tax-exempt foundation grants, the vast majority of progressive groups has become dependent on donors that strip them of their political impact, says Dudley. In dire economic times movement groups are faced with a devil's compact: they can have their bills paid or they can have their political freedom, but not both. When nonprofits became nonprofits, she complains, "we jumped out of the real world and into the sandbox." Newly relocated to Portland, she's working with the Working Families Party, which won status in 2006 to endorse candidates on the Oregon ballot. When the group started up, a dozen important local nonprofits were excited about the possibility of creating a people-funded party that would work for public financing of elections, single-payer health care, and sustainable economic growth. "Then they consulted their lawyers, who pointed out they'd be taking part in elections. That was it," she says. Rather than risking any threat to their treasured nonprofit status, the groups stayed away.

If entrepreneurial funders like the Rappaports and Sapersteins could or would help movement groups become self-sufficient, they'd really be building a movement. But they might also be threatening Democrats.

"None of this is new," sighs Karen Paget, the author of "Lessons of Right-Wing Philanthropy," a 1998 essay in *The American Prospect*. Paget, who worked in Washington in the early 1980s, recalls that after Ronald Reagan was elected, liberals were widely expected to learn from the Right and hit on a strategy for success. "People hoped after 1984, and again after 1994, that funders would understand that you can't parachute in every four years and jump-start grassroots progressive movements from scratch. We needed a change in approach then. It didn't happen." Paget was part of a group that made a concerted effort to move foundations to fund infrastructure building on the left in 1984. "Either they didn't get it, or if they did, they saw that kind of work as way too political." It remains to be seen if the latest group of liberal donors does, in the end, "think different."

Learning to Love
CHAPTER FIVE ☆ the Culture Wars

It is not possible to get around the present
to reach the future.

—BRIAN GREENE,
physics lecture,
spring 2006,
New York City

On election night in 2004, Justin Turner sat in a Cincinnati
bar and waited, feeling as if the fate of his new friends' lives
rested on the words of the TV news announcer. The rain
hadn't stopped all day, and looking around at the one hundred or so worn-out faces anxiously watching the election
results come in, Turner felt his chest squeeze tightly with a
mixture of hope and dread. As campaign manager, he'd seen
to it that the drive to repeal Article XII, a Cincinnati law
that literally legalized discrimination against homosexuals,
was about people, not about policy. The dread in his chest
came from his fear of letting those people down. The hope
that grew with each trickle of numbers from the precincts

was the hope that finally, after ten long years of failing, Citizens to Restore Fairness had hit on a message that worked.

In Washington, D.C., meanwhile, the TV prognosticators were testing their talking points. Halfway through the evening, verdicts on the 2004 election were already coming in. John Kerry and John Edwards had been defeated, several pundits declared, because of gays, abortion, and the so-called culture wars. The analysis was based on a single (flawed) exit poll that found that 22 percent of the country's voters cited "moral values" as their primary concern. In the days that followed, the "moral values" verdict became the defining story line of the election. Thomas Frank, author of the 2004 best-seller *What's the Matter with Kansas?*, wrote an op-ed in the *New York Times* that began, "The first thing Democrats must try to grasp as they cast their eyes over the smoking ruins of the election is the continuing power of the culture wars." In a crowded ballroom in Maryland a prochoice lesbian who'd worked her heart out for the group America Votes listened to liberal evangelical Jim Wallis, the editor of *Sojourners* magazine, blame the Democrats' defeat flatly on gay marriage and choice. On a conference call with contributors to the 527 group America Coming Together (ACT), Matt Foreman, executive director of the National Gay and Lesbian Task Force, which had turned out voters and trained key activists in several battleground states, heard Clinton consultant Harold Ickes sum up the race in a single sentence: gay marriage "lost us Ohio."

By the end of the week, the consensus was set and the pundits moved from diagnosing the problem to prescribing solutions for it. "The Democrats have become a party too dominated by social issues," wrote leftist *Nation* contributor Marc Cooper. Democrats need to turn their attention "away from culture and back toward class," wrote Alan Brinkley in the liberal *American Prospect*. The culture wars, wrote

Thomas Frank, are not about culture at all, "they are a way of framing the ever-powerful subject of social class," which is what Democrats must confront directly "with genuine economic populism." Jim Wallis described a nation split among three political options: "*conservative* on everything . . . *liberal* on everything . . . and a mix of the two, namely *libertarian*. Americans should quit them all," he advised, and leave "bifurcating politics of liberal and conservative, Left and Right," to open up a new "politics of solutions."

By January 2005 Thomas Frank's book about Kansas had stayed on the *New York Times* best-seller lists for more than four months; Wallis published *God's Politics: Why the Right Gets It Wrong and the Left Doesn't Get It: A New Vision for Faith and Politics in America* soon afterward. Frank had identified the problem—the Right plays bait and switch: "Vote to stop abortion; receive a rollback in taxes for the rich." Wallis advised changing the subject. "Many of us feel our faith's been stolen; it's time to take it back." Suddenly Democrats, liberals, and the traditional Left had found something they could agree on: conflict over cultural matters (like abortion, marriage, sexuality, secularism, and family lifestyle) was a trap dreamed up by the Right to distract good working-class people from their ruling-class enemies; liberals just needed to dump the culture war, get religion, and get down with blue-collar America again. As *New York Times* columnist Nicholas Kristof put it in a column published the day after the election, "To appeal to middle America, Democratic leaders don't need to carry guns to church services and shoot grizzlies on the way. But a starting point would be to shed their inhibitions about talking about faith, and to work more with religious groups."[1]

There's just one problem. As the late, great cultural critic Ellen Willis described in depth in her work, culture war by culture war is how American history has advanced. Fights over culture amount to fights over the constitutional promise of equality and freedom: freedom for whom and freedom to do what? To whom does the promise apply? Rarely has real change occurred because politicians polled the nation and adapted their views to please. If judges on the progressive flank had waited for civil rights to be culturally acceptable, we might never have legalized interracial marriage. Along with the books by Frank and Wallis, George Lakoff's work on reframing, or recasting, progressive messages hit pay dirt after 2004. But minority-led movements for social change have done more to reframe the way Americans think about themselves than any think tank or message shop. The civil rights movement was undeniably a major reframing enterprise (among other things). From three fifths of a man to gaining equal protection under the law, African Americans have transformed how Americans think about both race and humanity. Generations of immigrants have changed through their movements what it means to be a nation and a citizen, from melting pot to patchwork quilt. Transforming women from male property to near equals, feminists have overhauled the culture's gender frame. The LGBT movement has made huge advances in reframing love and family in just a few short decades: those same exit polls that showed that 22 percent of voters put "moral values" first also reported that nearly three times as many voters said they supported some form of legal status for gay couples (35 percent civil unions, 27 percent gay marriage).

The Bush/Cheney campaign framed Kerry as a flip-flopper on issues (they even deployed youths dressed in dolphin suits to dog him on the campaign trail), but what did him in were the lies about his Vietnam career that Kerry refused to confront. No single message did more to destroy his presidential chances than the so-called Swift Boat Veterans for Truth advertisements. But John Kerry is not America's first swift-boating victim. Think "gay agenda," think "welfare queen," think "racial preferences." Some Americans have been swift-boated for years.

When the Olin, Bradley, and Scaife foundations wanted to unleash an anti–affirmative action drive, they bankrolled a campaign that put on the ballot in several states a misleading measure that they called the Civil Rights Initiative. When one such measure, Proposition 209, passed in California, exit polling showed that 28 percent of those who'd voted in favor did not realize that 209 banned affirmative action. In 2004 a group calling itself Minnesota Citizens in Defense of Marriage sent so-called Truth Trucks around rural and suburban districts to target state legislators who had voted against a proposed amendment to ban gay marriage under the state constitution. The trucks carried large billboards emblazoned with the words "Want Gay Marriage? Vote Democrat this November."

The unfortunate thing about attributing the Democrats' defeat to the "wrong war" (culture rather than class) and the "wrong frame" is that it distances Democrats from the people and movements who've been fighting the culture wars for the last fifty plus years—the very people and groups who might help them. So-called culture warriors have spent decades in the Right's crosshairs, and they've learned a thing or two about swift-boating. Anyone from the AIDS activist group ACT UP could have told John Kerry that "Silence = Death." Most bullies don't stop just because you're nice to them. But the political calculus takes people of color, sexual minorities, and feminists for granted because they're unlikely to defect to Republicans. The result is that Democrats have limped through two elections hammered by the Right on hot-button issues like abortion and gay marriage, and the only strategic response they've come up with is to dismiss those issues—and those groups— as "special interests."

It's appealing to believe, as Thomas Frank does, that the "culture wars" can be trumped by talking about class or, as Wallis seems to, that one can flee false dichotomies by changing the subject. But the fact is, Democrats don't have a choice about whether to tackle gay issues or abortion or immigration. In this respect politicians find themselves in the same position as queer people: sticks and stones do actually break bones. You can take every high road all the way to the hospital, but it's better to fight back. In politics that means getting out front with a message that works—on class and national security, yes, and *also* on the "cultural" issues.

Before any more consultants tell him to fudge, the next Democratic candidate considering running for president would do well to talk to activists like Justin Turner of Cincinnati Citizens to Restore Fairness. Turner is not, by the way, a flaming queen. He's a thirty-four-year-old straight white man from New Mexico who graduated from Arizona State. His father was a county commissioner in Los Alamos. "Growing up, I watched how blacks and whites and Native Americans and Mexicans were treated differently. My parents just brought me up believing that if people were being treated unjustly, you were supposed to do something to change that." Nationwide he saw that gay people were being made into scapegoats. In Cincinnati the Restore Fairness campaign set out to prevent that. Turner was hired to design the field campaign. "What we wanted to do is get across the human impact of a policy," says Turner. And it worked.

From a skimpy minority of 32 percent who voted in favor of repealing Article XII in February 2004, the Restore Fairness campaign won over 53 percent of the vote on November 2. The campaign set a goal of turning out 60,000 supportive votes; the repeal proposition won with over 65,000. The gains came disproportionately from the most conservative parts of town. Four city wards, which had voted overwhelmingly to pass the discriminatory law twelve years before, shifted by as much as 22 percent. They voted for repeal even as they voted for George W. Bush. For twelve long years gay Cincinnatians and their friends had been trying to win support for repeal, to no avail. They had used an array of tactics, from comparing their enemies to Nazis to talking inoffensively about economic boycotts and the impact of discrimination on tax revenue. Nothing worked. Cincinnatians hated being called Nazis, but who, other than the chamber of commerce, was excited by getting into the nitty-gritty of taxes? In 2002, ten years after the law was passed, an anti–Article XII group headed by Gary Wright, in alliance with the city's largest civil rights organization, the National Conference for Community and Justice, settled on a campaign strategy that neither demonized or analyzed, but rather just talked about fairness. Starting two years before the proposition would appear on the ballot, volunteers knocked on Cincinnati doors and talked to whomever answered about what brings a city together and what tears it apart. They didn't ignore other things that were dividing the city (namely, racism and a series of police killings), but they also didn't shy away from the word *gay*. In their standard script it appeared four times.

"The key was to put a human face on the message and to address it head on," Turner told me on the phone from his home after the proposition passed.

Kerry campaigned in Cincinnati with the losing, instead of the winning, side. He brought onto the stage with him the one group of African American leaders that was *not* part of the Cincinnati for Fairness Coalition. In TV debates, he carefully parsed his terms, saying that he supported "civil unions" rather than "gay marriage," and went on to talk about all the goodies that unions would bring in the form of tax benefits. He did nothing to shift anyone's frame, or heart.

Although liberals today love to romanticize the 1960s, at the time Democrats kept their distance from the rebel movements that gave that decade its juice. By 1972 liberals were explicitly seeking to repackage liberalism as something less fiery. Gary Hart, who managed George McGovern's 1973 campaign, preached pragmatism. Speaking of the

1950s kids (the cohort now in party leadership), Hart said, "All of us are of a generation that, even though it is passionately involved, is not overly passionate. I worked for George McGovern because I was against the war. I never walked in a parade, never carried a sign, never broke a window. To end the war, you go out and organize precincts and elect the president who'll end it. You don't demonstrate."[2]

It's hard to move hearts without heart. Just as the GOP baits its base and switches, so do Democrats, who, just like the Right, use culture to distract. Packaging himself as the socially liberal alternative to the Right on cultural issues, President Clinton abandoned his base on the economic front, signing NAFTA over the objections of organized labor and environmentalists. When Bill Clinton appointed a task force on race, he adopted a very softly-softly approach to defending affirmative action, and appointed centrists, not civil rights activists, to "balance" the Right's appointments to federal courts. Having campaigned on a promise to defend gay rights, Clinton signed DOMA, the entirely redundant Defense of Marriage Act, which gave a shot in the arm to the bullies of the extreme Right and undermined moderate Republicans and Democrats.

What did all this bait and switch bring the Democratic Party? Two Democrats in the White House in forty years, the loss of the Senate, and then the loss of the House. It's no big mystery why. Those inconveniently irreverent and striving real people—whom pundits dare not mention by name but allude to with the code name "culture"—*those* Americans are the Democrats' base, whether the party likes it or not. Just ask any Republican. No amount of reframing or remessaging or plain ol' distancing will change that.

The truth is that Democrats, progressives, and fair-minded Republicans will never be antigay or antichoice or anti–racial justice enough to quiet their opponents. The only people left with any doubt about where Democrats stand on cultural issues are those whose lives are at stake—the Democrats' base. The culture advances at its own pace regardless. Immediately following 2004's supposed antigay backlash, Illinois and Maine passed nondiscrimination laws. California's legislature voted to gender-neutralize marriage—a first—despite Governor Schwarzenegger's veto. Massachusetts legislators upheld marriage equality. Connecticut passed a civil unions law. In the next months, Indianapolis and Topeka passed LGBT antidiscrimination laws. If grassroots culture warriors are doing this well while their leaders sell them out, imagine where the society would be if a big, powerful national party had actually put up a fight.

The LGBT movement has a word for a frame that's built around the fear of being honest: a closet. And there's only one exit: coming out. Coming out is a frame-shifter. Research shows that what most reliably melts a person's prejudice is a friend: knowing someone who is gay or supportive of gay equality erodes homophobia; living or working in an integrated place lessens racism. People who are clear about who they are, and who clearly respect themselves and their beliefs, attract respect. How many times have we heard that people vote for W not because they agree with him but because they know where he stands? At the age of fifty-seven, Lupe Valdez, lesbian Latina, was elected sheriff of Dallas in 2004. Valdez was the first woman, first gay person, and first Hispanic to be elected sheriff of Dallas, and the first Democrat to hold the job in twenty-five years. "Who would ever imagined . . . ," editorialized the *Dallas Morning News* after she scored her upset victory. A former prison guard and federal agent, the five-foot-two daughter of migrant workers was opposed by the unions that represented many of those working in the sheriff's department. She was outspent three to one. At the last minute her opponent, the favored candidate, raised alarms about Valdez's acceptance of campaign contributions from the

Washington-based Gay and Lesbian Victory Fund. How did she win? People in Dallas were ready for a change. Their Republican sheriff, a twenty-year incumbent, had just been indicted on charges of corruption. Valdez cast herself as an agent of change and made her sexuality work for her rather than against her. "I'm not like anybody in here. I'm the element of change. I'm a lesbian," she said. A third of those who voted for her were cross-over voters who didn't vote a straight Democratic ticket. Now Valdez is the only woman among 254 sheriffs in Texas.

After years of taking advice from consultants who urge caution and conciliation so as not to scare away anyone who might be undecided about their vote, Democratic candidates for high office, especially the presidency, seem almost incapable of expressing anything resembling genuine feeling. Commitment doesn't have to be synonymous with bullheadedness or insensitivity, but you do have to take a stand on something and explain your reasons for it. Valdez didn't win by obscuring who she was; she won by doing the opposite—by "coming out" and taking on her opponents.

Take a tip from former Houston mayor Bob Lanier. When opponents of affirmative action tried to put a Civil Rights Initiative modeled on California's on the local ballot, Mayor Lanier persuaded Houston's city council to change the wording. Instead of reading "The city of Houston shall not discriminate against, or grant preferential treatment to any individual or group on the basis of race, sex, color, ethnicity or national origin in the operation of public employment and public contracting," the proposition on the ballot asked, "Shall the Charter of the City of Houston be amended to end the use of Affirmative Action for women and minorities in employment and contracting, including ending the current program and any similar programs in the future?" Then Mayor Lanier talked forthrightly about what his opponents called "preferences." Critics of affirmative action have successfully framed the concept as the use of "quotas" to help undeserving minorities at the expense of "innocent" whites, especially white men. Lanier, a wealthy white real estate developer, appeared all over the city and on local television delivering the facts in a "good ol' boy" style that challenged the "reverse discrimination" illusion. "Let's not turn back the clock to the days when guys like me got all the city's business," he said. He reminded voters that "Anglo-male contractors got between 95 and 99 percent of the business before affirmative action . . . today they still get 80 percent." Houston voters defeated Proposition A by 55 to 45 percent.

Keeping their eyes on the polls, politicians tend to buy into the notion that no issue that appeals to only a minority of the electorate is worth staking out a position on. But even the most widely accepted progressive changes in America started out as marginal. Having the courage not just to stand up to the Right but *for* what is actually right can be a winner. As Deepak Bhargava of the Center for Community Change explains, "There's a view out there that only broadly accepted issues unite, but some of the most successful struggles in American history were led by minorities who were successful because they raised issues that moved people." Bill Lofy, communications director for the campaign training group Wellstone Action, starts his training workshops for candidates by telling a story about Minnesota senator Paul Wellstone (whose career inspired the program). "Wellstone, progressive Democrat of Minnesota, will be remembered forever as the man who, three weeks before he died, voted against invading Iraq, even at a time, in the fall of 2002, when his opponent was aggressively accusing him of being weak on national security." Polls told Wellstone a vote against war would lose him the election, remembers Lofy. But as Wellstone told the *Washington Post* two days after the vote, "I think people want you to do what you think is right. . . ." And he added, "How would I have had the enthusiasm and the fight if I had actually cast a vote I didn't believe in? I couldn't do that." Wellstone's vote resulted in a surge of support among Minnesotans that almost certainly would have led to his reelection had he and his wife, Sheila, their daughter, and three campaign staffers not died in an airplane crash.

"The compromise strategy doesn't work," Lofy told me after one workshop. The reasons are twofold: "If people are given the choice between a Republican and a Republican, they'll choose a Republican every time. And people are craving leadership that is real."

Support for discrimination is loud and easy to whip up, but it's shallow. In 2004 voters in eleven states approved anti–gay marriage ballot initiatives, but voting on an easily manipulated yes-no question is one thing; voting for a living and breathing legislator you respect is another. Across the states, proequality legislators won, regardless of race or party.

While John Kerry straddled the fence on gay marriage, every Massachusetts legislator who had voted for marriage equality won reelection. Promarriage candidates won six of eight open seats in the state house, and two proequality candidates actually beat anti-marriage incumbents. Typically, those who showed courage won out. Take Louisiana Democrat Melvin "Kip" Holden. As a state senator, Holden spoke out passionately and voted twice against a proposed constitutional marriage amendment even as he ran in a competitive race to become mayor of Baton Rouge. His opponent, Mayor Bobby Simpson, used Holden's votes against him in TV ads, but not once did Holden waver. He called it a matter of fairness and equality for all Louisianians, and on November 2 a majority of voters rewarded him. Kip Holden became the city's first African American mayor.

In 2006 anti–gay marriage amendments were on the ballot in eight states and were approved in seven, but opposition to the amendments topped 40 percent in five of the seven. Arizona became the first state to vote to reject an anti–gay marriage constitutional amendment (by a margin of 51 to 49 percent). Two pro–gay marriage governors—Deval Patrick of Massachusetts and Eliot Spitzer of New York—were elected by wide margins. Matt Foreman, executive director of the National Gay and Lesbian Task Force, said that fear mongering around same-sex marriage by the GOP and the extreme Christian Right "doesn't have the juice it had just two years ago."

The next war on the culture front is immigration. The debate about the economic impacts of immigration bypasses entirely what's really getting people riled up: the lurking suspicion that immigrants will make American culture change. Among callers who express fear around immigration to Air America Radio, that fear sounds to me to be less about losing jobs than about losing language; "no one speaks English anymore," even self-described liberals complain. Some have talked about the "Mexicanization" of American culture. Scapegoating is easy in Bushworld, and it's a great distraction from the real causes of anxiety like gas prices, low wages, and war. But culture fears won't be salved if Democrats, liberals, and those on the white Left talk only about immigrants' rights to work. Progressives have to come to grips with what citizenship means. Is it only the right to pull up a chair to the table? Or is it the right to change the table? This unsettling question lies at the heart of every culture war.

The good news is that plenty of Americans do have what it takes to fight the culture wars. Mostly they don't have the option of choosing complicity with bigotry or appeasement because their lives or their communities are at stake. In rural northern Oregon, Marcy Westerling watched the timber industry decline and dot.com businesses crash, followed by deep education cuts and soaring unemployment. Instead of focusing on government or corporate irresponsibility, conservative politicians redirected attention to what she calls "straw man" targets: gays and lesbians, feminists, and secular humanists. Westerling was all those things. Instead of caving in to the conservatives' advance, she formed a network, the Rural Organizing Project (ROP). "I was told again and again by urban progressive groups that there were two ways to be involved. One was to send my money to Portland, and the other was to drive in myself. But guess what? I like living in my town, and there are millions of people who like living in small-town communities who are willing to stand up," Westerling told *RadioNation* in June 2006. By drawing on the traditions that already existed in small rural towns, like church and town hall meetings, the ROP has organized get-out-the-vote and voter-registration drives and given voice to progressive citizens in more than fifty remote communities and small towns across the state. ROP volunteers go door to door, drawing on social networks. "At first you literally find people who are not feeling great about reactionary, exclusive politics. Then we develop a shared analysis." No handed-down position paper would have the same effect. The "frame" that ROP member groups (they call themselves Dignity Groups) chose for 2006 was "Rebuild America: The Gulf Coast, the Country, Our Communities." In advance of the midterm elections, ROP produced a voter guide that assessed each candidate's record in terms of those three elements. One piece of advice that Westerling reckons grassroots groups could share with Democrats is "throw out your experts!" The best grassroots groups get their advice and marketing for free by having a strong and empowered base that can help shape strategy.

Message shops rely to a great extent on type-casting groups and making extrapolations based on polls. As such, they can miss surprising allies that organizers turn up on the ground. When the immigration debate heated up after September 11, and the Right's propaganda asserted that immigration was not only a security threat but bad for business too, the Idaho Community Action Network (ICAN) visited local businesses and found that one hundred of them, in three counties, were willing to post pictures of the Statue of Liberty in their windows with the slogan "Immigration is an American Experience. Acceptance is an American Value." "We found that business owners didn't want a divided community any more than we did, and it woke us up," says Leo Morales of ICAN.

As a survivor of TV punditry, I know the value of a knock-out catchphrase, but as an infrequent media trainer, I'm also aware that for some the sound bite is a political Holy Grail. But not all political communication should be reduced to ten seconds or fewer. Ask Butch Callery, mayor of the small northern Kentucky town of Covington, officially one of the most open-minded places in the country. When Covington was considering an expansion of its human rights ordinance to cover LGBT people, city officials held two public meetings; nearly seven hundred people attended. And (according to the local media) when landlords and business owners expressed concerns, officials asked them to help draw up a law that worked for everyone. As a result, since 2003 Covington has been in the company of places like Berkeley and Beverly Hills: one of just a handful of communities across the country that ban discrimination based not only on sexual orientation but also on marital status and gender identity. Businesses and landlords caught discriminating three times against a person who's had a sex change or who dresses or looks like a member of the opposite sex can lose their license to operate in Covington and be slapped with a $100-to-$250 fine.

The "family values" discourse suggests that people's political views are like their religion: determined by deeply held beliefs, not subject to influence either by effective organizers or by their peers, or by access to analysis or facts. That approach comforts Democratic centrists who preach the urgency of going where voters "are" instead of trying to move them. But for far too long the Democratic Party has urged candidates to be what I call lip-synched liberals, cautious of speech, cut off at the heart. Hundreds of decent candidates have taken that advice—to disastrous effect. At the same time mainstream liberals, even progressives, have kept at arm's length the very people who know how to do the mind-by-mind work of talking to neighbors about tough topics.

Lip-synched liberalism is the strategy proposed again by those who call on Democrats to shift the debate from culture to class. What do they think culture is, anyway? Whoever decided to force a distinction between cultural and economic issues must never have suffered discrimination. It's a values-laden divide: in our society *culture* connotes something open to interpretation and optional; *economics* connotes the unavoidable hard-core stuff related to dollars and cents. Is discrimination on account of race social? How about failure to get a promotion because you're pregnant? When students are held back in school because of the way they look or the language they speak, which category does that belong to? As Left feminist Ellen Willis has written, "To dismiss as hallucinatory people's embattlement about what moral and cultural norms will govern their everyday lives and intimate relationships is to say that people (at least working-class people) do not, under normal circumstances, care deeply about anything beyond their paychecks.[3]

During the 2004 election many Democrats expressed a longing for "the real John Kerry," the young Vietnam veteran who returned from war and told the truth as he saw it to Congress. That Kerry participated in public hearings with other vets about the effects of service on those who served. The young man from Massachusetts wore his hair long and his jacket loose. He bonded with guys who not only threw their medals over the White House fence but also jettisoned generations of military tradition. They bared their hurt and spoke as "real men" (especially soldiers) weren't supposed to speak. Some cried. In public. They described the life-wrecking trauma of killing and torturing, and they expressed remorse. By dehumanizing the "other," they said, they'd diminished their own humanity. Some, like Kerry, walked into the hearing room with wounds or worse, many having been in military hospitals. Leaving the closet for society's savaged soldiers, vets left their private hells and, with their ugly stumps and missing limbs and signs of suicide attempts, came out. And they helped win official recognition for the condition called post-traumatic stress disorder. They shifted a frame. The nostalgia so many expressed for "that John Kerry" during the 2004 election was a desire not just for a man with political "spine," but for, I would argue, a culture warrior.

CHAPTER SIX ☆ Not by Spin Alone

> "Our legislature is full of well-meaning people, but this year, not only did they decline to increase the minimum wage (again), but they refused to consider regulating the use of cell phones by teenage drivers because it would be too much 'government.' Yet they voted to impose their own morality on any and every pregnant woman in South Dakota, practically without regard to individual circumstances. It seems to me our 'ship of state' has been blown pretty far off course."
>
> —THERESA SPRY FOR STATE SENATE, South Dakota[1]

Charon Asetoyer cares about language. Ever since she founded the Native American Women's Health Education Resource Center in Lake Andes, South Dakota, in 1988, she has been trying to persuade outsiders that one-size-fits-all slogans don't. They certainly don't fit her people, the Comanche, or the tribe she married into, the Yankton Sioux. But three weeks away from a yes-no vote on an explosive abortion ban in South Dakota, Asetoyer didn't care what language was on the "vote no" signs. She just wanted to see some signs.

"We woke up this morning, and there are 'vote yes' signs all over the county. Big signs, yard signs, signs with women's faces in patriotic pink and blue. This is not good," Asetoyer e-mailed her friends.

One of her friends wrote to the vote-no campaign (headed up by South Dakota Campaign for Healthy Families), which was trying to overturn the abortion ban. "Does Healthy Families have any 'vote no' signs we could use in the First Nations? A bunch of signs would be most useful," the friend suggested, adding that a voter-turnout drive was planned for the area.

The answer came back: "So sorry. The campaign has no signs, nor any immediate plan for them."

Journalists tend to be fascinated with political speech (a distant cousin of their own profession) more than with the nuts and bolts of field organizing, but political campaigns are not won by messaging alone. In the wake of the Democrats' 2004 defeat, as we have seen, an ocean of ink was spilled on the discussions of public relations, spin, and "framing." Subconscious mental "frames" affect the way a listener thinks and feels in response to words, linguistics professor George Lakoff explained in his best-selling book *Don't Think of an Elephant!*[12] Lakoff traveled the country advising progressives to "reframe," or reposition their policies linguistically, to make them more attractive to America at large. Foundation grants were awarded, and new public relations groups were set up. But nothing changed the fact that as the side favoring the criminalization of abortion plastered South Dakota with its messages on the eve of a landmark vote, the "vote no" message was almost nowhere to be seen. As Asetoyer's friend wrote in an e-mail: "No *darn* signs. WE HAVE NO SIGNS."

For all the talk of framing, it's not the frame around what Democrats say that needs to change; it's what's Inside the frame and the mechanism that exists for communicating the message.

In February and March 2006, the South Dakota legislature passed and GOP Governor Mike Rounds signed an abortion ban, HB 1215, that criminalized abortion in every instance, with no exception for rape or incest, and no exception for the woman's health or, for that matter, the health of the fetus. South Dakota rallied, gathering thirty-eight thousand signatures to put what then became Referred Law 6 on the ballot. Come November voters had to vote yes (to uphold Referred Law 6) or no (to repeal it). The group responsible for the ballot initiative campaign was the South Dakota Campaign for Healthy Families, directed by Lindsay Roitman.

When we talked in October, Roitman was in her office in Sioux Falls, a half day's drive east of Asetoyer in Lake Andes. She had nothing against signs per se; what drove her decisions were money, time, and electoral calculus, she told me. Given a limited amount of the first two, the third determined the shape of the campaign. Roitman arrived from Seattle (where she left a job in the corporate headquarters of Starbucks) and set up shop in Sioux Falls in July. The first thing she did, she explained, was hire a team of professionals to conduct focus groups to get the lay of the land. A self-described liberal, prochoice Democrat, Roitman said she was "taken aback by some of the attitudes we found," but at the end of the day "we chose to respect the minds of the people of South Dakota rather than run a huge visibility campaign." Instead of mounting a big education drive, the campaign, which was bipartisan, set out to identify every potential no vote in South Dakota and concentrated on getting those folks to the polls. "That's what I can do. I can turn out those votes," said Roitman. "I can't correct years of failure in just four months with two million dollars."

When Roitman arrived, South Dakota boasted just one small statewide women's organization: Democracy in Action, whose core group consisted of twenty-five to fifty members. NOW (the National Organization for Women), National Abortion Rights Action League (NARAL) Pro-Choice America, and the Feminist Majority had no significant presence except on college campuses. Planned Parenthood operated two clinics, but only one that conducted abortions. The clinic was tucked away in a squat windowless building on the outskirts of Sioux Falls, and a doctor flew in once a week from next-door Minnesota.

What slogan did the "vote no" campaign settle on? "This Law Simply Goes Too Far." Roitman explained that it targeted all those South Dakotans she'd found in focus groups who opposed abortion but felt Referred Law 6 was too extreme. The strategy seemed reasonable in the short term, but what if the ballot measure won, and the ban's supporters returned with an amended version, with a rape or incest exception tacked on, I asked her. "November 8? We can't be focused on that, unfortunately," she said.

The Right has rhetorically outflanked the prochoice movement, hijacking the words *family* and *life* and *human* to devastating effect. But the movement has outpaced its opponents in other ways too. The Right hasn't advanced by language alone, but also by lucre and organizing and lies. South Dakotans describe a situation not so different from the one described by Thomas Frank in *What's the Matter with Kansas?* As jobs and resources have trickled out, the Christian Right and its antigovernment allies have poured in. In the last thirty years Theresa Spry, a Lakota mother and grandmother living in the far western part of the state, has seen her hometown, Rapid City, lose jobs, health care centers, quality public schools, and money for public services of any kind. By the time the backlash movement showed up, it was like a tide flowing onto a bulldozed plain.

Thirty years ago South Dakota probably had some forty or fifty family planning clinics, several offering abortions, remembers Spry. She worked as a family planning counselor "until the environment for that kind of work became too severe," she told me. "The Religious Right walked in the door and took over," she says. "Over a decade evangelicals took over the school board, the city council, the county commission, the legislature." HB 1215 wasn't passed overnight. Indeed, in 2004 Governor Mike Rounds vetoed a bill that was very similar to HB 1215, but new bills just kept on coming.

It's the same across the country: those on the Right and the Left don't just have different political views; they do politics in different ways. The money on the liberal side floods in and out with the election tide, focused on the White House, Congress, the Supreme Court, or, as in the case of South Dakota, an emergency like an all-out abortion ban on the ballot. Abortion rights groups are not outspent. Abortion rights groups gave more than $1.4 million in the 2004 election to candidates for national office. In addition, Emily's List raised $34 million in 2004 and $2.5 million in 2006 for female candidates who support abortion rights. The National Right to Life Committee, the largest electoral outfit on the criminalization side, raised and spent only about $1.7 million in 2006. But the opponents of abortion rights sow their grass roots year-round through their networks of right-wing churches and state-based women's organizations, including Eagle Forum and Concerned Women for America. The U.S. government also helps out. In fact, Leslee Unruh, campaign manager for the antiabortion Vote Yes for Life on Six campaign in South Dakota received a lot of support from U.S. taxpayers whether they know it or not.

The Alpha Center occupies a former Planned Parenthood clinic in a mall in Sioux Falls. Founded by Unruh, Alpha advertises free pregnancy tests, but they come with fierce antiabortion messages. The Abstinence Clearinghouse, also founded by Unruh, pushes abstinence-only sex education and abstinence until marriage. In 2005 Unruh's Alpha Center received $300,000 from the U.S. Department of Health and Human Services. The clearinghouse's tax returns list more than $1 million in government funds in 2003 and 2004. In 2002 Congress awarded the Clearinghouse $2.7 million to create national standards for abstinence-only curricula for use in schools across the nation. In July 2006 Citizens for Responsibility and Ethics in Washington (CREW) filed an IRS complaint charging that through her advocacy work, Unruh had violated the terms of her organization's tax exempt status. Unruh denies that she lobbies on the public dime, but there's no denying her frequent appearances in Pierre, South Dakota's capital, advocating for the abortion ban.

The pressure has been on South Dakota's citizen legislators for years. Even before the no-exceptions abortion ban, South Dakota had passed laws granting full legal status to the fetus and imposing all manner of restrictions on women seeking to abort. HB 1215 was only one of five new bills passed restricting abortion in 2006 and in 2005, the state passed a law requiring doctors to tell women that abortion ends the "life of a whole, separate, unique living human being." (A federal appeals court blocked the enforcement of that law in October 2006 on the grounds that it crossed the line from science to ideology.)

What was happening on the other side during all this time? I ask Spry, who replies bluntly, "What other side?"

Women's rights advocates (the "other side") do exist in South Dakota, but they face more challenges than most. With a total population of some 750,000, South Dakota has one of the smallest and most rural state populations. Sixty-five percent of South Dakotans live outside of metropolitan areas; communities are scattered, and resources are slight. According to the U.S. Census, almost 90 percent of the population is white, and Native Americans are the largest minority, between 8 and 9 percent. (The reality is probably above that.) The state ranks fiftieth in the nation in earnings for women, and women here are the least likely women anywhere in the United States to own a business or work in a professional job. Only 16 percent of state legislators are women, compared with 22 percent around the country. According to the Centers for Disease Control, 47 percent of South Dakotans report having had sex in high school. Nationally 16 percent of female teens report having unprotected sex, but even without the ban, South Dakota had one of the lowest rates of abortion in the United States—5 per 1,000 women ages 15–44 compared to the national rate of 16. By every indicator Native Americans have it the worst: higher levels of poverty, violence, and rape, and less access to health care. Native Americans have nearly double the infant mortality rate of whites (11 percent compared to 5.4 percent). In 2006 only one Native American woman sat in the state legislature.

As soon as the legislature passed the abortion ban, national prochoice groups, which hadn't been active in the state for years, responded with condemnation and national fund-raising appeals for their groups. Prochoice South Dakotans—helped by Planned Parenthood, NARAL Pro-Choice America, the ACLU, and NOW—sent money to the Healthy Families campaign, but while imported organizers scrambled to map their territory and come up with a campaign, the national right-to-life movement didn't have to move; it had been in place all along, growing its strength over more than a decade. In state primaries in 2006 evangelicals challenged moderate Republicans in seventeen races around the state and won every time. Half the Republican state senators who had opposed the ban were ousted. "We are witnessing the birth of the Evangelical Republican Party . . . God's Party," wrote a local columnist. Even as Republicans at the national level publicly downplayed what was happening in South Dakota, the national abortion-criminalization movement was treating South Dakota as a priority.

On the Democratic side, the party of South Dakota was cowed, as it had been for more than a decade. In 1992 Democrats dropped from their platform any commitment to a woman's right to choose. Six out of ten Democrats in the state senate and seven out of nineteen in the house voted *for* the no-exceptions abortion ban. Come convention season, while Republicans were making abortion a central theme of the race and conservative advocacy groups were pledging their help in dollars and volunteers, the Democratic state leaders discouraged candidates from making abortion any kind of issue and approached the midterm elections in a decidedly low-key manner. They mounted no coordinated campaign, for example, and developed no plan for a large-scale get-out-the-vote or voter-protection effort. The one independent prochoice advocate—Kate Looby, South Dakota director for Planned Parenthood—was asked to leave the state party convention. (Looby was the only representative of any prochoice organization present.)

While the "vote no" message was cautious to the point of camouflage, the "vote yes" ads were aggressive to the point of lying. I watched the Healthy Families campaign TV ad twice before I realized it was against the ban. Hoping to appeal to those "Goes Too Far" voters, the Healthy Families campaign ran a TV ad that began, "South Dakotans agree: honor and protect human life, reduce the number of abortions." The "vote yes" ad that got the most airtime featured a group of doctors claiming that the ban did make exceptions for women who have been raped (it didn't; inaccessible morning-after contraception is not the same thing at all). Eventually the ad was pulled.

State senator Bill Napoli, an outspoken supporter of HB 1215, appeared on national television, where he was asked by a PBS reporter if he could imagine any circumstances in which a doctor might be permitted to carry out an abortion. He thought for a moment, then said steadily, "A real-life description to me would be a rape victim, brutally raped, savaged. The girl was a virgin. She was religious. She planned on saving her virginity until she was married. She was brutalized and raped, sodomized as bad as you can possibly make it, and is impregnated. I mean, that girl could be so messed up, physically and psychologically, that carrying that child could very well threaten her life."[3]

It was hard to say which was most disconcerting—Napoli's utter lack of concern about message discipline—or the possibility that his disturbing vision might actually reflect his movement's message.

It'd be nice to write South Dakota off as some sort of heartland aberration. While South Dakotans are farther down the road, the country is headed in the same direction. The conversation about abortion needs to change, but the top-down message strategy is only a tiny piece of a much larger problem. Lynn Paltrow, founding director of National Advocates for Pregnant Women, described it to me this way: "For a long time most of our organizations did a terrific job focusing inside the courts. Once a bill is passed, they're right there to challenge it. But the intrepid grassroots activists—like Asetoyer and Kate Looby—are out there on their own. There's just not been a whole lot of support for state-based organizing."

In 2000 Theresa McGovern, former director of the HIV Law Project in New York City, received a grant to study women's health advocacy efforts in several states. What she found corroborated Paltrow's comment. Three decades of right-wing activism have restricted women's access to reproductive—or any kind of—health care. Across the board, women of color are the poorest, the most limited in access to health services, and the least hooked into national advocacy networks. Abortion rates are down, due to the closing of clinics and to laws criminalizing doctors and various procedures. And health care providers have felt the chill: they're afraid to engage in the political process—including offering testimony to legislators or talking to the media—because of the violence that some extremists have directed against their profession. Reproductive health care has become controversial, and the more associated with national "prochoice" groups local activists are, the more controversial they become. "People from New York, pardon me, can undermine the efforts," one activist told McGovern. Isolated from the very community that could support them, advocates at the legislative level work primarily on the defensive.

Bamboozled by talk about values voters' having caused the Democrats' defeat, Democrats got busy after the 2004 election reframing their messages on abortion. John Kerry came out of the gate calling on the Democratic Party to recruit and elect more prolife candidates. Howard Dean pledged to make the party "more welcoming" to prolife voters. Hillary Clinton dusted off her husband's phrase about keeping abortion "safe, legal, and rare" and took it one step further, calling abortion "sad, even tragic." Chuck Schumer, chair of the Democratic Senate Campaign Committee, handpicked antichoice Democrats to run for the Senate in Pennsylvania and Rhode Island. (Bob Casey Jr. won; Jim Langevin withdrew in favor of a victorious pro-choice Democrat.)

Eight weeks before the 2006 election, which political party was touting its efforts to reduce abortion in the United States? Democrats. In September House Democrats put forward a proposal, the Reducing the Need for Abortions and Supporting Parents Act. It promised to reduce the number of abortions by one million over the next decade by increasing funding for pregnancy prevention and contraception, as well as funding for the infant nutrition program. In a concession to the Right, the bill also required abortion providers to notify patients of procedure risks, a provision that prochoice groups had fought on the grounds that it opened a door to yet more policing of doctors and intimidation. The bill's supporters included Representative Rahm Emanuel, a Democrat from Illinois and chair of the Democratic Congressional Campaign Committee; Representative Harold Ford, a Democrat from Tennessee; Bob Casey Jr.; and Senator John Kerry.

That same week at Pepperdine University (one of the country's leading conservative colleges), Kerry emphasized his commitment to making "abortion rare."

To Kerry's comments, a representative of Focus on the Family Action said, "Whenever you talk about making abortion rare you're really missing the moral point, that a wrong can never be right." Where the

Right's going next, I would argue, Democratic voters and the majority of Americans don't want to follow.

Having come out victorious in 2006, Democrats run the risk of misinterpreting the midterm election results as a vindication of their reach-out-to-the-Right-and-grieve abortion strategy. The trouble is, the Right isn't going away. As fast as Democrats reach to the Right, the Right darts farther still. A step farther down this path, contraception is murder too.

The Democrats' narrow electoral strategy may win votes and power in the Congress, but it plays havoc with women's lives. Prochoice politicians have made a lot of common ground with abortion foes already, and it's resulted in a tidal wave of laws policing not just pregnant women seeking abortion but all pregnant women, and conferring rights on fetuses. Restrictions on access to contraceptives and comprehensive sex education are already changing what kids learn in school and which contraceptives pharmacists sell. Over the last few years, pregnant women have been arrested and jailed in South Carolina, New Mexico, Arizona, Alabama, Colorado, Georgia, Missouri, North Dakota, and New Hampshire on the charge that they were child-abusers even before they gave birth. Most of these women had untreated drug or alcohol problems, but demonizing "bad" women is just a start.

The Democrats believe it's only pragmatic to talk about abortion as tragic and rare; in South Dakota, they call it "respecting" South Dakotans' views. But paying all that respect to those who would criminalize abortion is the opposite of standing up for women, their doctors, and their advocates. As McGovern's research shows, attitudes toward abortion spill over onto those who conduct the procedure, endangering the doctors, isolating those who defend them, and demonizing the women they serve. Reaching out to the "prolife" movement, Democrats are weakening their own.

Lynn Paltrow believes the conversation has to change, not so as to "respect" abortion foes, but to show some respect for women, and the truth about their lives.

"It's not as if there are two groups of women, women who give birth and women who have abortions. They're all the same women, and they're all being hurt by lack of health insurance and lack of respect," pointed out Paltrow at National Advocates for Pregnant Women in New York. According to the Alan Guttmacher Institute, about 6.4 million women become pregnant each year, but about 1.29 million choose to abort. The single focus on abortion doesn't encompass the bigger picture. "If the way you talk and the way you act leaves out too many people—if it leaves out women of color, if it leaves out women who want to carry to term, if it leaves out women who want treatment for addiction and can't get it—how can we possibly build the organizational and political strength that we need?" The Democrats' decision to link access to abortion to broader health options, therefore, is a good one. But the "make abortion rare" part is problematic.

"I feel very strongly that the way we talk about things does matter, and it matters because you can either inspire or not, convert or not, motivate or not," said Paltrow.

In the three decades since abortion was legalized in 1973, some women's groups have gone from talking about liberation and self-determination to talking about more abstract things like "privacy" and "choice." The National Abortion Rights Action League (NARAL) has even changed its name to NARAL Pro-Choice America to cut that nasty word *abortion*. When it comes to messaging, framing, and finding common ground with abortion's foes, the women's movement has been there and done what some Democrats are recommending now, and they've found that filing down principles for the sake of politics has cost them, as well as American women. The price has been flagging movement momentum and shrinking rights. *Roe* remains the law on paper, but as the broader concept of "choice" has shriveled, so has the women's movement. The two phenomena are related. According to a report from the Center for the Advancement of Women, fewer women belong to women's organizations today, they're less active, and they skew older. Minority women—specifically African Americans (63 percent) and Hispanics (68 percent)—when polled, express a stronger wish for a movement than white women (41 percent). Yet white women continue to lead the largest women's organizations. And the younger the woman, the less likely she is to belong to a woman's group or to call herself prochoice. A poll in South Dakota showed that voters under thirty approved of the no-exceptions abortion ban two to one. (The Zogby poll should be taken with a pinch of salt, as it was funded by the Christian Right.)

The scene is bleak, but there are reasons for hope. In 2004 women's rights groups almost fell apart over language. They reframed and pulled off the biggest march in D.C. history. NARAL Pro-Choice America, the Feminist Majority, Planned Parenthood, and NOW put out the call for a March for Choice in 2003. Women-of-color-led groups balked. "Choice has been a contentious word from the start of this movement," said Loretta Ross, director of the SisterSong collective, a national federation of women-of-color-led health organizations, from her office in Atlanta.

Different women's "frames," if you like, are different. White, middle-class, and upper-class women have through history been denied the right to choose an abortion; their priority is to secure and protect that right. Throughout the same history African American women, Native women, immigrants, and the poor have been denied the right to "choose" to reproduce. Generations of Native women and others were subject to sterilization abuse. "By calling their demonstration the March for Choice, NOW, NARAL, Feminist Majority, and the rest were reopening old fissures," explained Ross. The member groups of

SisterSong demanded that the name of the demonstration be changed back to the March for Women's Lives and demanded as well a shift in message. Loretta Ross became cochair of the rally and ensured that the literature used for organizing and the media placed reproductive health and rights within a broader social justice context, a frame Ross has called "reproductive justice." On April 25, 2004, the March for Women's Lives became the largest march in the history of Washington, D.C. Although D.C. police decline to release crowd estimates, individual police officers familiar with similar events estimated that over a million women and their supporters took part.

In terms of diversity, the young women's group Choice USA is turning itself around from the inside. "You have to replenish those on the front lines," says Kierra Johnson, the development director. "If polls show a decline [in support for reproductive justice] among the young," says Johnson, "who's going to fight and be lawyers and providers and serve in the legislature down the road?" It's exactly the question the Democratic Party has been asking itself, and the party could do worse than consider how Choice USA answered it. Founded in 1992 by Gloria Steinem and others, Choice USA looked at the polls in the late 1990s and decided it had to overhaul itself or die. If it was to keep to its mission—empowering young women—its operations had to change. While national Democrats (not just the Kerry campaign) continue to believe that campaigning for a twenty-first-century American majority with an overwhelmingly white, virtually all-male leadership is just fine, Choice USA believes a group's inside and outsides have to match. Says Johnson, "We're committed to diversity and youth empowerment, and we work so that at every level our demographic reflects the movement we want to see."

Choice is bigger than *Roe vs. Wade,* says Johnson. "A lot of people are uncomfortable with choice, and that doesn't mean they're prolife or pro–legislating limits on women's access." The group needed more than a shift of message; it needed a shift of thinking and power. In 2001 Choice USA hired Crystal Plati, at twenty-seven the youngest executive director of any national women's organization. Johnson, who just turned thirty, came on board that same year. Says Johnson, "Those who are the most threatened are the most likely to fight. It's absurd to leave them on the sidelines. But if you're telling them they have the smarts and responsibility to lead, you have to let them lead."

The challenge is not to put abortion in the closet, say activists like Johnson, but to put it in a broader context. "That means saying access to abortion isn't enough. . . . You have to address stigma, economic barriers, and what those mean for service providers."

Unfortunately, finding common ground with abortion foes has usually meant acquiescing to the Right. Is the Democrats' shift in message going to revitalize their base? I asked Eveline Shen of Asian Communities for Reproductive Justice (ACRJ). Shen and her organization got very involved in the successful fight against Proposition 73, a parental-consent initiative on the ballot in California's 2005 special election. A similar ballot initiative was defeated *again* a year later. Traditional Planned Parenthood affiliates in California mobilized their lists of identified prochoice voters, but those lists didn't include new voters, new citizens, or nonvoters who nonetheless cared about young people's rights and reproductive health. Shen and her organization reached out to local grassroots groups in the San Francisco Bay Area and brought medical experts in specifically to talk to Asian communities about the impact on families when young people are dragged into court for failure to acquire parental consent.

Language is important, says Shen, but having the networks and the credibility in place is more important: "The Democrats and the reproductive rights movement can say whatever they like, but if they don't have the connections to the communities, it'll make no difference."

The Ms. Foundation for Women has recently started a Reproductive Rights Coalition and Organizing Fund specifically to put resources into local communities and the states. National women's rights groups, which tend to believe that having their own affiliates in the states is sufficient, have pushed back. But as Terry McGovern's research has shown, the networks of the national advocates tend to be isolated both from health care providers and from those who most need services. "It's not as easy as reworking a national message," the Ms. Foundation's Desiree Flores told me. She visited the group La Voz Latina at the southernmost tip of Texas and asked about the stereotype that Latinas don't like to talk about abortion. "It's not that they don't want to talk about abortion," she concluded. "It's that they don't have access to transport to get to a clinic for a Pap smear or a blood pressure test. You can't silo abortion off by itself." When a woman has no doctor, talking about a "private decision between a woman and her doctor" makes no sense.

Wyndi Marie Anderson, who directs a fund that offers small grants to women who need assistance to pay for abortions in South Carolina, believes that abortion is, already, too rare. "I know that because I turn away women who want grants every year," she says. It's not a sentiment that goes down well in her meetings with prochoice Democratic Party activists in Washington. Another thing that drives them crazy, she says, is when she brings up class. Women are the majority of the U.S. population and the majority of U.S. voters. Poor white women, specifically poor women without a college education, have been leaving Democratic ranks for twenty years. "Framing and messaging . . . I hear a lot of my colleagues talking about how to talk to people. I immediately step into the role of the people they're going to be talking to—and find it insulting right away," says Anderson.

"I may not be educated, and I may not be shopping at Whole Foods, and I may not be driving a Prius, but when you pull up at my door and you've been told by some [liberal pollster] how to talk to me, I know what judgment is . . . and I know when you think I'm dumb and I'm not listening to anything you have to say."

Anderson went hoarse trying to persuade Democratic Party activists that it was their language, not their principles, that needed an overhaul. Democratic Party materials don't need reframing so much as they need rewriting, suggests Anderson. "They need to write those things in language my family back home can understand." In her meetings with beltway advocates seeking her advice, she urged them to bring in literacy experts to make sure party materials weren't written in language beyond the sixth-grade reading level. "But nobody ever wants to do that." The Right did it. In 1975 Republican activist Alan Crawford edited the monthly *Conservative Digest.* In his account, Crawford recalls that *Conservative Digest* was designed to appeal to lower-middle-class Americans "of the Wallace constituency," as well as to traditional conservatives. "There would be no fancy prose or big words," he reports. Letters from readers praised the writing as "easy to read." "We made valiant efforts to appeal to the working man."[4]

Democrats face a problem not only of message but of messenger, says Anderson. "But then it also gets into, are we into having a democracy with a whole bunch of different kinds of people? Or are you wanting to brainwash people with one specific kind of message?"

It's hard to find a slogan that fits everybody's reality, but it's even harder to get majorities to support slogans that just don't ring true. The valuable contribution made by the messaging debate is the recognition that, as George Lakoff has written, people's internal "frames" are different. "We all have a metaphor for the nation as a family," Lakoff wrote in *Don't Think of an Elephant!* Conservative language and policies tend to appeal to those who operate under a "strict father" frame (top down, absolute, inflexible). Liberal politicians and their programs appeal to those who see the world through a more "nurturant parent" lens (egalitarian, permissive), he explained.

Lakoff is hardly the first person to contemplate the topic. Frankly, feminists have been doing it for decades. For some reason, when a Berkeley linguistics professor talks about people being "different"—on the Left and on the Right—it's called "messaging." When women, people of color, and gay and lesbian people talk about the same thing, it's disparaged as "identity politics."

Wishing that progressives shared a single common frame, even about simple concepts like family and parenting, doesn't make it happen. Consider Lakoff's notion of the family. It's a catchy idea that aspires to bring people together, but the truth is, just about everything about nationhood, family, and parenting is culturally particular. "We have Founding Fathers," writes Lakoff, but I'll bet that when he was enslaved, abolitionist Frederick Douglass didn't think of the founders as his fathers. "We send our sons to war," Lakoff continues, but that "our" is open to interpretation. American trade unions talk about "sons" when they speak of "the sons of labor," but when they fought in colonial wars, organizers like Eugene Debs talked about workingmen's sons fighting not in their fathers' but in their bosses' wars. Family in America is a complicated affair. Segregationist Strom Thurmond had a daughter by his African American lover—was she family? Was Thurmond, who paid secret hush-money to her mother, nurturant? What about when he was preaching "segregation forever" even as he crept into his black lover's bed?

The debate over message gets at half of the challenge—namely, that speakers need to think about the people they're speaking to. But the necessary partner to that thought is, you need to know something about those people. In Lakoff's work, there's rarely a mention of race. He barely mentions gender. It's rather like talking to South Africans and pretending apartheid never occurred. Americans of voting age today grew up on one side or another of a color line. Lakoff can talk with confidence about the Right, but ask about race or gender or sexuality, and he comes off rather like a fish asked about water; he seems befuddled. When asked about how the Right's messages manipulate deep-seated gender and racial prejudices, Lakoff typically responds by saying more research is needed. But patriarchy and white supremacy are hardly unresearched topics, nor are they details in America; they're at the heart of why our society looks and behaves the way it does. The Right's rhetoricians seem to know precisely where the hot buttons are—calling Democrats "girlie men" in 2004 worked like a charm, as did an anti–Harold Ford ad in 2006 that featured a white woman cooing at Ford (who is black): "Call me, Harold."

It's not good enough to rely on guesswork. Lakoff, for example, is interested in the Right, and so he went to the trouble of attending Religious Right gatherings. But Democrats and national advocacy groups share a habit of thinking that centralizing money and then shipping out last-minute organizers works. It doesn't. For one thing, the organizers don't know the territory; for another, it's tricky to guess.

In 1998 Washington state, where 85.3 percent of the population is white, faced an anti–affirmative action intiative (I-200). The pro–affirmative action campaign focused on women and directed its messages at women voters. It spent the vast majority of campaign time and money targeting white women, but the message all but ignored race and African Americans. To the surprise of many experts, the campaign failed and I-200 passed, garnering 58 percent of the vote, including 51 percent of white women's votes. DePaul University professor Sumi Cho looked at the data and discovered that white women enjoyed the lion's share of economic benefits from Washington's affirmative action plan, but they so feared that affirmative action (benefiting people of color) would injure the interests of their husbands and their sons, that they voted yes on I-200. The campaign "failed because pollsters and political consultants severely misjudged white women's interests," wrote

Cho in a law review paper. White women in Washington voted white before they voted female. In 2006 pro–affirmative action forces in Michigan adopted a very similar strategy to defeat an affirmative action ban in their state, and voters approved the ban 58 to 42, with 59 percent of white women voting in favor.

The Democrats' "make abortion rare" reframing concedes an awful lot of territory to those who've been legislating away women's rights since the day *Roe* was decided. It gives up on the idea, for example, that a woman's right to make her own reproductive decisions is her private right. Period. Moreover, while Democrats shift their seat on the field, the field keeps moving. And abortion is not just, as George Lakoff and others have called it, a "stand-in" for other issues. It's a life-saver for women who want and need abortions. Real health services, not "stand-ins," and real doctors are under assault. And the action isn't in Washington, D.C. It's in the states. By the time a battle reaches the capital, it's already way too late. Critics of *Roe v. Wade* often make the case that "prevailing opinions" have changed in the years since the case was decided. The more state legislatures pass laws restricting women's rights, the more those critics have to point to as evidence of the shift they seek.

The motion away from the rights promised in *Roe* isn't driven by pressure from the top of the national political scene; it's driven from below, in the states, where harried lay legislators, like those in South Dakota, come under pressure from well-organized forces with a vision (albeit a twisted one, if Napoli is any indication) on one side, and hear only cowed whispers from the other.

Even one powerful politician who declines to stand up for women's full, comprehensive health care rights on principle is one less ally for local advocates like South Dakota's Theresa Spry. What sort of difference would it make if Spry had big-name help at her back, the way Napoli has James Dobson and the whole Focus on the Family empire?

In Kansas, prochoice organizer Julie Burkhart runs a Political Action Committee: ProKanDo. What we need, says Burkhart, isn't more reaching out; we need more standing firm. "If we're going to take this issue away from the Right, we have to do it now and do it methodically and think about the future," she told me. "What we need are leaders who'll stand on principle, leaders who'll stand up."

Not long ago, Burkhart watched a media frenzy start around a murder that the Right was seizing on to stir up support for an Unborn Victims of Violence Act (UVVA) then pending in the Kansas legislature. A fourteen-year-old girl, Chelsea Brooks, had been killed by her twenty-year-old boyfriend. Brooks was nine months pregnant. Abortion foes responded by framing the entire case as an example of violence against an "unborn victim" and reason to pass the UVV law.

"In the past I've testified [about] the implications of giving a fetus the same rights as a child, and I've seen eyes glaze over. It just doesn't resonate," says Burkhart. In this case she rejected the Right's frame. Burkhart's own sister was killed by a battering boyfriend. She decided to write an op-ed for the *Kansas City Star* about Brooks's murder and her sister's, and she made the women's killings the issue that the community needed to talk about. "Almost immediately the press changed," says Burkhart. The next day's coverage talked about the murder of Chelsea rather than the death of the fetus, and a local TV station followed up with an investigative report on violence against women and girls. "Legislators even called me," Burkhart told me, sounding vaguely surprised. "After the first coverage of Chelsea, they were ready to throw in the towel on UVVA. Given some different talking points, they snapped out of it," she says.

Legislators wouldn't pass half the bad laws they do if they weren't so bullied on the one hand, and so ignored on the other, believes Burkhart. "If we don't give them a different way to think about things, what do we expect?"

Burkhart formed ProKanDo in 2002 to help grow support for pro-choice prowoman candidates at the state and national levels, and to educate voters and legislators. In Kansas that meant supporting Kathleen Sebelius in her successful bid for governor that year (and again in 2006), and opposing Attorney General Phill Kline, who became famous when he subpoenaed the medical records of women and girls who received abortions in his state. Burkhart's group produced and distributed a voter guide that queried every candidate about where they stood on everything from comprehensive sex education to abortion to insurance coverage for contraception. Sebelius won reelection by a huge margin (58–41) in 2006, and Kline went down to defeat by almost the same margin (42–58). But ProKanDo didn't stop there. Before the 2007 session, as it does every year, ProKanDo will hold presession workshops for incoming state legislators, "so they actually know about the issues they're voting on," explains Burkhart. The group doesn't dodge the tough stuff. In 2007 the ProKanDo workshops will focus on late-term abortion, a particularly demonized procedure that the Supreme Court is due to rule on, one of the first cases taken up by the current court.

"I doubt if any of these legislators have ever heard anyone speak about it from a personal perspective, and they appreciate the opportunity," explains Burkhart. She intends to bring doctors and women with firsthand experience to the capital to meet with legislators. "We can't be afraid to talk," says Burkhart. "If we don't talk, who will?"

In the 2006 election campaign, the chairman of the Democratic Senate Campaign Committee, Chuck Schumer, is reported to have established what he called a twenty-four-hour rule. According to the *New York Times,* "If Republicans ran an advertisement attacking a Democratic candidate, a response had to be on the air within 24 hours."

Lynn Paltrow believes that's just what's needed on the reproductive health front: "We need to respond to every lie and present our full version of what the truth is, every time, not meet in the middle, because the middle keeps shifting right."

One of the big stories on a big-news night for Democrats, November 7, 2006, was the defeat of the South Dakota abortion ban. "No" voters outnumbered "yes" voters 185,934 to 148,664. Defeating the ballot measure by such a margin was sweet victory for women's rights' advocates. But it may be short-lived. Leslee Unruh of the Yes for Life Campaign responded to the verdict almost immediately by saying she expected similar campaigns to take place in states including West Virginia and Texas, and she pledged to return to the South Dakota legislature too: "They're never going to win, and we're never going to quit."

Lindsay Roitman wrapped up the ballot amendment campaign hoping that the Campaign for Healthy Families group would stay in place. "Had we been organizing more aggressively for longer, we might never have faced this," she told me shortly before the vote. Others, including Native activists Charon Asetoyer and Theresa Spry, believe more could have been done this time around if the campaign had focused on building a movement instead of winning a single political campaign. The campaign's office failed to respond to phone calls after November 7, but according to its report filed with the South Dakota secretary of state, the organization entered the last week of the race with close to a quarter of a million dollars still in the bank. The money could have been spent on a public education campaign on reproductive rights broadly, believes Charon Asetoyer—not to mention "Vote NO" signs in Indian country.

"Healthy Families did not understand the politics in our community, so how could they make assumptions about how we would vote?" Asetoyer wrote to me later in November. In the last weeks of the race,

Asetoyer received enough funds from a small nonprofit to pay for inexpensive ads in well-read local newspapers. When billboards appeared on Pine Ridge Reservation declaring "Children Are Sacred. Vote YES on 6," she and her colleagues distributed posters that stated, "Women Are Sacred. Vote NO on 6." Their message read, in part, "All women deserve to be safe from violence, and all children deserve to be wanted. Tell the legislature to promote comprehensive Sex Ed in our schools, tell them to work to reduce domestic violence and sexual assault. Tell them to feed the hungry children we see every day. Vote NO on 6 and tell our elected officials to take care of families." On Election Day, Native "no" voters outnumbered "yes" voters on Pine Ridge 64 to 36 percent. "Healthy Families missed a huge opportunity to build a strong and diverse political organization," said Asetoyer. It's an organization prochoice South Dakotans are going to need going forward.

The South Dakota abortion ban was defeated, but the legislators who voted for it were not. Just about all the prochoice Democratic women running for office lost (nineteen out of twenty-two, with one going into a run-off). Every antichoice woman incumbent prevailed. The antichoicers hold as much power as they ever did. Theresa Spry ran for the state senate in 2006, winning a four-way primary, but she went down to defeat in the general election against Bill Napoli, the man who babbled on PBS about unmarried Christian virgins and rape. Now Napoli's headed back to the senate, where a new abortion law with some exceptions is said to be in the works.

Spry has run for office before, and she'll do it again, she says, because it's not just the law, it's the legislature, that has to change. "We can't give up. We just need a long-term plan," she told me. "There's a long-term plan on the other side. What's ours?"

Megaphones for
the Masses

I got
Two turntables and Coltrane
And not just blue Coltrane
And not just Monk and not just Miles
I got
A million musicians
Playing over my head
A band of angels
Responding to a percussion of stomps and hollers.
Heads don't even know what's happening to them,
They just know that something is happening to them.

—CARL HANCOCK RUX

During the 2004 election season Kerry/Edwards supporters called in to my show on Air America Radio seeking yard signs. All I could think to do was to direct these callers to the Kerry campaign website. Finally one exasperated caller protested that she could find no darn way to obtain a yard sign through www.johnkerry.com. The caller was right. I went online and checked, live on the air, and it made for discouraging radio. Not only was there no apparent way to obtain a yard sign through the Democratic presidential nominee's national campaign website, but there was no obvious way to do much of anything besides make a dollar contribution and sign up to receive e-mails (which would ask for yet more donations). The state Democratic parties and coordinated campaigns were even worse. Shortly after November the independent group Grassroots Democrats surveyed state Democratic parties and found that half had no website of any sort. No state party's website provided downloadable sign-up sheets for activists to use when tabling or during voter-registration drives. Only three states offered downloadable organizing guides, and they were unreadable: 50 to 83 pages of turgid instructions. In the last weeks of the 2004 election campaign, I took to encouraging signless callers to pick up a hammer and make their own darn sign. (I may appear to be obsessed with political signage. I'm not; I'm simply reporting what I hear. Signs, it turns out, are a very big deal. Especially when they're all coming from the other side.)

I thought of Kerry's dispirited yard-sign seekers later, in February 2006, when the senator from Massachusetts explained that one reason the Democratic message fails to connect with the public is that Democrats have a smaller "megaphone" than the Republicans have. "Our megaphone is just not as large as their megaphone, and we have a harder time getting that message out, even when people are on the same page," Kerry complained to the *New York Times*.[1] The senator is undeniably correct when it comes to right-wing talk radio, pay-to-say pundits, Fox News, and the editorial pages of the *Wall Street Journal*. But blaming the media is lame when your own people won't provide the tin-can communication tool of front-yard partisans. In some parts of the country the one-dollar yard sign is the most effective medium for miles around.

Democrats aren't strapped for cash. Every four years they spend hundreds of millions of dollars on political advertising, almost two thirds of it on network TV. After all that advertising spending, they emerged from the 2004 election with nothing to show but their scars. Republicans and the Right, on the other hand, spend those same advertising dollars (together the parties spent an estimated $2 billion in 2004), but they *also* invest in another veritable empire of influence. Long before the arrival of "new media" the Right already had plenty of "old media." In fact, by the mid-1990s the Right already had enough ideologically aggressive media to shuttle consumers along a communication conveyor belt that spanned if not cradle to grave, then close to it. From the plethora of right-wing campus newspapers (*The National Review, The American Spectator,* and *The Weekly Standard* are all available free to graduates), to internships for indoctrination-friendly journalism students, to stipends at well-endowed think tanks for intellectuals, the Right has created a system for recruiting and training talent, enough to communicate, 24/7, in much, much more than stereo. If a Limbaugh-listening "dittohead" seems to live in a different world from your average liberal, it's because he does. And not just the dittoheads: as late as July 2006, 50 percent of Americans still, still, *still* thought there were weapons of mass destruction in Iraq. (Just to be exceedingly clear: there were none. *None.*)

The Right enjoys freedom of the press not only because its attack-flacks have effectively intimidated and cowed the so-called mainstream but also because it owns its own media, and lots of it. If your views lie to the left of Newt Gingrich, on the other hand, you're lucky to make a fly-by appearance as a punching bag on a talk show controlled by your opposition. On Capitol Hill no Republican member of Congress need miss a vote or break a sweat in traffic on his way to a far-flung studio to appear on TV. Paul Weyrich, founding president of the Heritage Foundation, has seen to it that Heritage has its own inhouse broadcast-quality radio facility. In the 1990s, before Fox, the Right had its own America's Voice studio, in a reconstructed townhouse near Union Station, close to the Senate and House office buildings. The last time I ventured to America's Voice, Weyrich's portrait smirked down from a wall in the reception area. His lips seemed to move: "Lowly lefty, enjoy your minute of airtime, we've picked the topic, we've framed the terms, we own the studio; you are our prey." No longer needed when Fox hit its stride, America's Voice closed up shop at the end of the decade.

Hamilton Fish of the Nation Institute (a progressive think tank) puts it this way: "As far as Middle America is concerned, information is under siege. Every primitive prejudice is enforced, every disaster played up, and the rest is a flood of human interest pabulum. Into that, when you slap on the screen another 'Operation Freedom' headline, it's bound to be met by an uncritical response." Trying to break through with an alternative worldview in a thirty-second, or even an eighteen-minute, appearance in between commercials is like trying to joust with oncoming cavalry from your wheelchair.

In eight years in office, the Clinton administration not only did nothing to correct the tilted media playing field, it participated in shoving the tilt more sharply toward pabulum and the Right. Even when Democrats controlled Congress and the White House, the leadership did nothing to restore the fairness doctrine, which required broadcasters to dedicate time to public affairs and to air a variety of views, not just those they agreed with. The elimination of the doctrine, by the Federal Communications Commission under Reagan, opened the door for Rush Limbaugh and around-the-clock, one-note, wingnut talk radio. The presence of a Democrat in the White House did nothing to insulate public broadcasting from corporate pressure or from red-baiting by Republicans in Congress. (Media reformers have never received any meaningful support for their smart proposal to fund the Corporation for Public Broadcasting directly through a tax on TV advertising, as is done in the U.K.) What's worse, Bill Clinton signed the Telecommunications Act of 1996, which loosened already slack limits on the number of media outlets a single company could own in a community, exacerbating a bad trend toward corporate consolidation. After lobbyists from the tel-com industry were finished wining and dining lawmakers, the Telecommunications Act might as well have been called the Media Monopoly Act. The media-merger frenzy that followed left the American public with fewer TV and radio options, less news, and a range of opinion that stretched from the center to the right, then farther right. Clinton's FCC also approved the "great giveaway" of the new digital broadcast spectrum: when new frequencies became available thanks to digitization, the FCC simply gave away publicly owned broadcast resources worth tens of billions of dollars. That is, in 1997 it handed out billions of dollars' (now hundreds of billions') worth of the people's airwaves free to private companies, no strings attached, for those broadcasters to use mostly to make money. The FCC might as well have given the corporations a free ride over to the U.S. Treasury to simply print themselves money.

With friends like this, who needs Rupert Murdoch? Clinton/Gore saw to it that the White House went online in 1994, and a Democratic Party website was launched soon after. In that year, by contrast, the GOP had not only a website but a national, shared database. Throughout the 1990s Republicans were developing voter-list-sharing technology and political websites—known then not as blogs, but as "me-zines." (Patrick Ruffini, the webmaster for Bush/Cheney 2004, started his own me-zine in 2001.) Already by 2002 every Republican fieldworker in every state had access to a shared national online voter file. The Republican National Committee even pimped its ride: Reggie the Registration Rig, a fifty-six-foot customized truck, complete with fold-out stage, Xboxes, video screens, and all the gear needed to enlist new voters, showed up at college football games, Cinco de Mayo celebrations, WrestleMania, and NASCAR races. On the Democratic side, at the level of media and outreach, old guard and new guard tussled for turf, and mostly the old guard won. In an era of interactive communication, www.JohnKerry.com was used mostly as a one-way mechanism, dispensing talking points and opportunities to donate money and sign up, but offering little opportunity for users to communicate.

It was left to innovative party outsiders to produce some of the greatest hits of the 2004 campaign. Hollywood producer-director Julie Bergman produced with actor Will Ferrell a short video called *White House West* for America Coming Together (ACT). In the video Ferrell impersonates the president. It was released on the Internet, with a tag urging viewers to check out the ACT website. The video garnered millions of hits online, as well as free airings on news and entertainment TV shows, and made the front page of the *New York Times* Sunday "Arts and Leisure" section with the headline "The Democrats Get Their Funny Bone Back." According to Bergman and ACT, 33,000 citizens thereafter volunteered to work for ACT in battleground states. "They didn't expect this," recalls Bergman, who believes the campaign could have done more with other video clips distributed by Net-savvy individuals. (A two-minute cartoon lampooning both Kerry and Bush put out by JibJab.com received ten million viewings in a month—three times the number of hits on both presidential campaign websites.) But ACT declined to expand the project, no reason given.

Half a decade after cable TV viewers began to outnumber broadcast TV audiences, the Kerry campaign still shunned cable TV. According to the New Politics Institute, cable outpaced broadcast in audience share back in 2001. Commercial advertisers long ago made the leap, shrinking their ad-buys on the networks and pumping up cable. But Kerry/Edwards didn't. (In 2004 less than 2 percent of all campaign ad dollars were spent on cable by both parties together, almost all of it by the GOP.) The disdain for cable makes no sense unless you are a media consultant like Harold Ickes. Ickes, Bill Clinton's former deputy chief of staff, headed up ACT's media arm, the Media Fund, in 2004 and received (as all campaign consultants receive) a commission from the campaign. If a campaign spends $2 million on TV time, the consultant who produced and placed the ad receives 10 to 15 percent—that's $200,000 to $300,000—on top of that, from the client. It works for the consultants, but it doesn't work for their clients, the Democrats. (You don't get a dime, by the way, for putting up a yard sign.)

At the dawn of the television age Marshall McLuhan coined the phrase "The medium is the message." Fifty years later the medium is also the messenger. How a candidate chooses to communicate can say as much about that person as what he or she chooses to say. In the last few election cycles Democratic candidates have stated their intentions to attract young voters, for example, and they've researched messages they would convey but they've typically ignored the ways young people actually communicate.

"It's just so frustrating," says Malia Lazu, who served as the national field coordinator for the Young Voter Alliance, a collaboration of seven youth groups that coordinated efforts to increase young voter turnout in battleground states. The reluctance to invest in cable TV advertising is typical: "Democratic consultants resist the very strategies that work every day for commercial advertisers," Lazu told me. "They'd rather blame the consumer for not paying attention than go to where the consumer is. They'd never get away with that in advertising."

Ninety percent of blogs are not political, and yet candidates need to get their messages there too. "The candidates are not in people's lives, not even on a first date, let alone at a point where you can ask a person out to do something on a Tuesday," Lazu protested. "Just sending the Kerry kids out to campaign for the youth vote is simply not going to cut it." During much of 2004 Lazu was a participant in the Showtime original series *American Candidate*, where she mounted a presidential campaign for herself and finished second in a national call-in vote tally. Today she directs the Racial Justice Campaign Fund at Progressive Majority, an organization that trains up-and-coming candidates.

If the Democratic National Committee wanted to reach the progressive part of the hip-hop generation, it could hire Bay Area deejay and hip-hop entrepreneur Davey D. He's built up a following on his radio shows and his website, which mix political talk with politically conscious hip-hop music. Now he's broadcasting direct to cell phones. He told me that two years ago he approached a slew of progressive broadcasters with the idea of cell-phone radio, but no one was interested. Now his listenership is growing, and the biggest media corporations are hot on radio and video-messaging via cell. Republican policies aren't down with the people, but their PR strategies are, Davey D told me; as long ago as 2002 he observed that Republicans were doing a better job of following urban media habits than Democrats. During the California gubernatorial recall election, he says, he'd turn on the radio late. "On most urban radio stations, the two A.M. commercial block shows up at two-forty A.M. If your club gets out at two A.M., forty minutes later you're in your car driving. The first commercial you hear should be a political ad. I told the people in the Democratic Party this. They looked at me like I was crazy. You can get those two A.M. spots for fifty bucks." Did he see any such ads? "No. They're out of touch."

In the run-up to the 2004 presidential election, Davey D estimates that "there were at least eight mixtapes and compilation songs released encouraging the hip-hop community to go to the polls." The participants ranged from artists like Wyclef Jean to Jadakiss to Eminem to WC and Mack 10 to Cypress Hill to scores of underground artists who participated in what they called the Slam Bush project, a series of national hip-hop contests designed to attract new voters to register and vote. The project had no help whatsoever from any of the Democratic campaigns or consultant-driven 527s. "The Democrats have not made any serious investment in young voters or hip-hop voters," Davey told me at the second Hip Hop Political Convention—a gathering of progressive hip-hop activists in Chicago in August 2006.

But savvy use of youth-oriented media has great potential. When Ned Lamont was running for the Democratic nomination for U.S. senator from Connecticut, he put blogger Markos Moulitsas in a TV spot aimed at young people, which bloggers also posted on the video website YouTube. People were talking about it and playing it to their friends long after Lamont stopped paying for airtime.

In England, some districts permit voting by text message. In the United States the president doesn't send text messages to voters reminding them to vote, but that's just what happens in Italy. Now that over half the U.S. population owns a cell phone, the Bay Area techies behind the nonpartisan and nonprofit group Mobile Voter believe the future lies in text-message activism. It worked in South Korea, where activists used "Txt power" to help elect a human-rights-activist president. In the run-up to the 2006 election, Mobile Voter in collaboration with Music for America set a goal of registering fifty-five thousand young voters at concerts via mobile text messaging. At the end of the day, they'd registered half that number.

Apart from young voters, the Democrats' other most reliable base is minority voters, but the consultants at the top of the party haven't shown much interest in the media those groups use either. According to recent data, ethnic media reach 51 million Hispanics, African Americans, Asian Americans, Arab Americans, and Native Americans—almost a quarter of all American adults. Of these, 29 million (13 percent of all adult Americans) not only use them regularly but favor ethnic media to their mainstream counterparts, reports Sandy Close, director of New America Media, a consortium of some 750 newspapers and media (radio and TV) serving various ethnic and immigrant communities. The Kerry campaign spent barely a penny on ethnic media. While the Bush campaign, apparently encouraged by George W. Bush himself, broke tradition to pursue minority groups through their media, Kerry/Edwards waited until late in the summer to announce a $3.5 million ad-buy in black and Spanish-language media. (More than thirty Asian-language media responded with the message "Kerry to Asians: You Don't Count.")

The DNC and the Democratic campaign committees claim to care about expanding their vote among immigrants and Spanish speakers, but being out of touch still trips Democrats up. Shortly before the 2006 congressional elections the Democratic Senatorial Campaign Committee had to pull an online ad after Hispanic groups protested the inclusion of a shot of people scaling a border fence in a montage of fearful images that included Kim Jong Il and Osama Bin Laden. And Sandy Close reported that as of late August 2006 "not a dime has been spent during the midterm elections on Spanish language advertising by prime-time candidates—at least that I know of in California or New York. I see no great push to build constituencies among the 'ethnic/minority/immigrant' populations, despite a lot of lip service."

For the last few decades, *make your own darn sign* is pretty much what fed-up Democrats have been left to do, and in the past five years, thanks to a lot of new technology, all that do-it-yourself sign-making has re-

ceived a boost from the mainstreaming of the Internet. Now all the talk
is about the blogosphere. Website by website, e-mail by e-mail, fed-up
(FU) Democrats are dragging their party into the twenty-first century.

FU party activists haven't created a megaphone—they've created a
parallel party message-and-mobilization machine. Small Democratic
donors are giving directly to the candidates of their choice through online sites like ActBlue.com, while a laterally networked activist base
known as the netroots is sharing information, ideas, and strategy
through live-time chatrooms and group discussion sites, or blogs sometimes hosted by teams of bloggers. As long as the Internet is "free," no
one needs a studio or a license to broadcast or send mail. Most Internet
sites are underwritten by volunteers and user contributions. A handful
attract enough advertisers to make a living. (Bloggers offer advertisers
an easy way to reach a very targeted and Internet-savvy audience.)

The most high-profile of the races backed to the hilt by the blogs in
2006 resulted in defeat: the Senate race of Ned Lamont of Connecticut.
Ned Lamont, whose name recognition was zip at the start of the year,
rose to national prominence in a few short months thanks to what the
New York Times described as "a blogger uprising" mostly from outside
the state. As the bloggers themselves are quick to point out, to see only
the effect of the netroots is to miss the context in Connecticut. Keith
Crane is the founder of DumpJoe.com, the first website to float the idea
that Connecticut senator Joe Lieberman could—and should—be un-
elected. Way more trucker than typist, with big hands and a bad hip,
Crane says he had never touched a computer before 2003 (he still types
with one finger), but in Lamont circles he is hailed as the man whose
website sparked a successful David versus Goliath primary challenge
to three-term incumbent Lieberman, Wall Street's favorite Democrat.
As they waited at the Sheridan in Meriden for the votes to be tallied on
primary night, strangers clapped Crane on the back and reached out to
shake his hand, but Crane was quick to deflect credit. "It wasn't me, it

wasn't the blogs, it was the voters of Connecticut who did this," he told everyone who would listen. "The sooner we dispel the myth that bloggers are all radical outsider teenagers, the better." Crane says he resorted to the Internet only after trying his darnedest to work within his party. As a Democratic Town Committee member in Branford, Crane tried for years to get his fellow Connecticut Democrats to see that Lieberman could be beat. "We could see his vulnerabilities even when the party refused to see it."

Like many Connecticut Democrats, Crane and his blogging partner, Edward Anderson, had been fed up with Joe Lieberman for years. The senator refused to relinquish his Senate seat when he ran for vice president. (Had he won, the state's Republican governor would have been able to appoint his replacement.) He voted for Bush's war on Iraq and with the GOP just about every chance he got. Lieberman, in Crane's estimation, wallowed in the rewards that came from sucking up to insurance companies and corporate lobbyists. (Although right-wing journalists loved to criticize Lamont's "outsider" support from Internet activists, no senator receives more corporate PAC donations from out of state than Lieberman. His wife, Hadassah, worked for Big Pharma's favorite public relations firm, Hill and Knowlton, before she resigned in early 2006.) When Lieberman voted to confirm Alberto Gonzales as attorney general, Crane and Anderson finally had it. They began a grassroots campaign to recruit a primary opponent, started their website, DumpJoe.com, and got out into the streets. DumpJoe.com featured a photo of the Judas-smooch that the president laid on Lieberman after a State of the Union speech. "The Kiss," as it was known, showed up on hundreds of red buttons that Crane and Anderson handed out by the sackful. And a massive papier-mâché sculpture of the two heads locked lip-to-brow showed up on a truck that bird-dogged Lieberman's campaign around Connecticut. "The Kissmobile drove the Lieberman campaign nuts," Anderson chuckled, showing off the pictures on his cell phone on primary night.

Bloggers helped recruit a candidate and rally the volunteers and cash to make a primary contest seem like a viable prospect. When a thousand volunteers signed up online—from every municipality and town in Connecticut, Tom Swan, Lamont's campaign manager, was persuaded that their passion was real. "We asked the netroots if they were serious, and they proved they were," Swan told me. On primary night a small room across the corridor from the newspaper reporters' space was jam-packed with twenty or thirty bloggers from around the state and the nation. They piled their equipment onto tables littered with power cords and cables and (in stark contrast to the print journalists, who silently pecked at their keyboards across the hall) chattered. They're a collaborative mob. "Who can crunch the numbers? What are they saying about turnout?" Far away from Meriden, bloggers like Markos Moulitsas in Berkeley and Matt Stoller in D.C. were picking up the locals' talk and pushing it out on their nationally read blogs. As everybody in Connecticut was quick to point out, Lamont's state-based energy was fueled and fanned by national bloggers. MoveOn.org raised more than $250,000 for Lamont nationwide. (The organization claims to have about fifty thousand members in Connecticut.) "About 146,000 voters gave Lamont his upset victory to Lieberman's 136,000. So even if only half of MoveOn.org members voted—a conservative estimate, given their typical turnout rates and deep involvement in this race—they would account for Lamont's margin of victory," reported *The Nation*'s Ari Melber.[2]

Losing the primary, Lieberman went on to run, and win, as an independent. Ned Lamont's 52–48 primary win didn't shatter the earth, but it sent shock waves through the Democratic establishment. The spectacle of a rump-group revolt against Al Gore's former running mate not only drove the Lieberman camp crazy, it threw the establishment media into hysterics. Lanny Davis, former Clinton White House counsel and a Bush appointee, penned a *Wall Street Journal* op-ed in defense of Lieberman in which he compared "the hate and vitriol of bloggers" to Ann Coulter and Joe McCarthy. Conservative columnists too railed against a "liberal inquisition" and attacked "Ned's nutcases" and "crazies." Mort Kondracke, a fixture on the nation's most vitriolic news network, Fox News, wailed that Lieberman's defeat could mean the end of "civility in American politics." At the same time the Connecticut showdown provoked awestruck talk in progressive circles about the potential for progressive revolution at the netroots of the Democratic Party. Some said that at last some progressives had found the means to make an end run around the centrist establishment of Clinton and the DLC, and, by so doing, shove the whole edifice in a more healthy direction, in the same way that, thirty years earlier, right-wing activists had taken on and transformed the GOP into the extreme-right outfit it has become in Bushtimes.

Establishment media love to play up conspiracies and play down community activism, but the success of the Lamont primary campaign lay in its closeness to the ground as much as in its presence in the blogosphere. "It's not the media alone. It's never the media alone," Tim Tagaris, a former Marine sergeant who left the DNC to direct Lamont's web activities, told me.

"There's the real hero of tonight." Crane gestured to the stage just before the victory hoops and hollers broke out. Up on the dais was a burly-looking guy in a crumpled T-shirt and a baseball cap worn backward. "Tom Swan. He's the real kingmaker in this place."

Swan has been an unconventional campaigner since long before the birth of the Internet. As executive director of the Connecticut Citizen Action Group (founded in 1971 by Connecticut native Ralph Nader), Swan perfected the art of the pointed political stunt. "There was the hot tub outside the state Capitol . . . and the armada of boats filled with chanting protesters that followed an apoplectic Senate Republican leader, Lou DeLuca—and the lobbyists he was entertaining—down the Connecticut River," reported the *Hartford Courant.* Team Enron trading cards showed up under windshield wipers at one of then governor John Rowland's public events, as did a "Bad Santa" that belted out mocking lyrics to "Rudolph the Red-Nosed Reindeer" at a GOP holiday dinner, reported the *Courant.*

It wasn't Markos Moulitsas, it was Swan who won one blogger over to camp Lamont. A writer who goes by the tag "Larkspur" at MyLeftNutmeg admitted, "To confess, it was because of Tom Swan that I jumped on the Lamont Campaign bandwagon early this year. It wasn't the blogs or Markos. It was because of Tom Swan. I knew that Tom was one of the best progressive field organizers in CT."

"The angry masses must be mobilized," wrote Nixon's speech-writer Patrick Buchanan in 1975. "The time has come to seek out, not avoid, political conflict, with liberals of both parties." The new Right advocated "confrontation politics."

Buchanan saw the journalist as Machiavellian. In Democratic circles, the closest equivalent so far to the new Right's crop of advocate/journal-ists are the bloggers and their readers, the netroots. In the election cycle of 2006, netroots activists organized support for twenty candidates who started out very much as long shots. For months they sent money, atten-tion, and advice their candidates' way. Seven, including two senators, Jim Webb of Virginia and Jon Tester of Montana, won; far more lost. But the point, said Kos, wasn't just to win, it was to open the process. "When we chose our candidates for the ActBlue netroots list, the candidates weren't even second tier. They were all third tier or worse. The point of adding them to our page wasn't to win, it was to expand the playing field, help build a fifty-state national party, and work to build for the future."

What kind of future do the liberal bloggers have in mind? It's not that obvious.

"They want to make me into the latest Jesse Jackson, but I'm not ideological at all," Markos Moulitsas told *The Washington Monthly* in 2006. "I'm just all about winning."[3]

The bloggers and their netroots readers want access to a party that until now has shut its members out. Looking at the last few elections, the bloggers reckon they could do a whole lot better at a whole lot of things than the candidates they've been voting for. "We have no interest in being antiestablishment," Matt Stoller, a blogger at the popular site MyDD.com, told *In These Times*. "We're going to be the establishment."

Their bluster has been taken for radicalism, and the blogs have criticized some Democrats (most notably Joe Lieberman, but not just him) for yielding too much to the GOP on taxes and the war on Iraq and other issues, but their critique is generally more nuts-and-bolts pragmatic than programmatic. It's how the party and the Democratic candidates are doing things that seems to get bloggers riled up more than, say, anything related to the party platform. MyDD.com launched an entire online discussion group dedicated to screening candidates' TV ads and grading them, providing a smart, free "focus group" for ad-makers. But when Bill Clinton agreed to meet with a group of bloggers in his Harlem office, they came away from the meeting flattered. Liberal bloggers love to vilify the centrist DLC, which Clinton once chaired, but once this group met the man in the flesh, they wrote glowing reports about his "openness" to a dialogue. What the dialogue was about they didn't say (in fact, most of it was off the record, a proviso to which the bloggers agreed). Those in attendance at the Clinton meeting, who represented most of the most widely read political blogs on the Democratic side, were uniformly white and male—a fact that became a topic of debate in and of itself in the Democratic blogosphere, as well it should. (When blogs are criticized for lack of diversity, Markos Moulitsas has typically said first that he's Salvadoran, and second that anyone can start a blog who wants to.) The bloggers' strategic thinking doesn't seem to focus on the benefits (not even the strategic ones) of putting concrete effort into multiracial blog-organizing.

Moreover, bloggers' candidate choices are idiosyncratic, based on expedience more than on principle. Bloggers loved antiwar contender Ned Lamont in Connecticut, for example, but only after months of being pestered did MoveOn.org even conduct a poll of its New York members on the question of whether to endorse Jonathan Tasini, an antiwar Senate candidate who was running against Hillary Rodham Clinton. On the very night when antiwar Lamont was celebrating in Meriden, Representative Cynthia McKinney was defeated in Georgia. McKinney was one of thirteen Democrats who had not only opposed the war but had actually voted for Representative Jack Murtha's plan to withdraw troops when Republicans pushed Democrats to a bluff-calling vote on the floor of the House. Bloggers who were wild for Lamont had little to say in defense of McKinney, who had been threatened with a lawsuit but never indicted after a messy dispute with Capitol police (whom she accused of racism).

When the Right's Paul Weyrich, Patrick Buchanan, and Grover Norquist took aim at the Republican Party's elite, it was to skewer its weakness and firm up its principles. The Democratic insurgents aspire to do the same, but so far they have prioritized electing Democrats generally and beating up on media that mistreat Democrats. When a current event threatens to reveal or expand a fissure among Democrats over policy, the most influential blogs tend to become awfully quiet awfully fast. When Israeli warplanes were destroying Lebanon's civilian infrastructure in response to the kidnapping of two soldiers and the killing of three others in 2006, DailyKos and MyDD weren't talking about it; nor was MoveOn. The bloggers were as shamefully silent as the Democratic leadership itself. (Some bloggers said they didn't know enough about the topic, but a lack of information has not typically held bloggers back.) When tens of thousands of immigrants marched in the streets of Illinois, Wisconsin, Florida, Texas, New York, and California, they dominated the local TV news but not the liberal websites. (In Dallas, Chicago, Los Angeles, and many other cities, these protests were the largest in the cities' history.)

The media attention that was indispensable to the immigrant rights marches of 2006 came not from the liberal, left, or independent media—but from the most traditional sort. A massive walkout by tens of thousands of high school students in Los Angeles was apparently organized by text message, but Spanish-language TV giant Univision and commercial radio hosts did the most to swell the numbers and inform the crowd of their rights in the streets of this country's biggest cities. "Economic opportunity [was] combined with political urgency," says Roberto Lovato, an immigrant rights-organizer-turned-journalist. Looking to serve their market better, hosts on some of the least political stations around urged their listeners to turn out and even suspended normal programming to give information to marchers. "The rock stars of the immigrant rights movement aren't bloggers or network TV anchors. They're deejays," says Lovato. Soon after the spring marches, one of the most popular Spanish deejays in the country, Renán Almendárez Coello, "El Cucuy," went out on a two-week tour around the United States called Votos por America to get Latinos to register before the midterms.

When it comes to changing the media landscape (or trying to), not all of the action is in the blogosphere. In 2006 the National Newspaper Guild did something very twentieth or even nineteenth century: the union attempted to buy a chain of newspapers on behalf of its workers.

The Guild made a bid on twelve properties that became available after the breakup of the Knight-Ridder newspaper chain. Linda Foley, Guild president, says the idea had been around for a while, but the time seemed right. She believes the union came pretty close to acquiring at least two of the twelve—the *Philadelphia Inquirer* and the Philadelphia *Daily News*—before being outbid by a private company. "Bidding made us a real player. We'd never even been in the game before," Foley told *RadioNation*. Although they attracted little national attention, the NNG bids made local news, engaged community activists, and put a focus on the importance of workers and local ownership. "Reporters were pushing our talking points about media consolidation and workers in chains," said Foley with a laugh. In a pretty grim time for newspaper employees, workers were excited to see Guild representatives touring their plants as prospective buyers. Besides, local newspapers aren't so expensive, and with cross-promotion in other media, Foley thinks they could be financially viable. Newspaper workers have little to lose. "If we didn't make ourselves players, the negotiations would happen around us, and our members would be left to pick up the pieces of their lives," Guild leaders said; "we can either sit at our desks, or duck under them, or do something." Look out for more bids on local papers from the Newspaper Guild.

If you're looking for other media that build movements, you'll find some in the fields, literally. A megaphone doesn't have to be high-tech to be effective. Woodburn, in the Willamette valley in Oregon, houses the state's most concentrated population of immigrant farmworkers and tree planters. Talk about a megaphone: the Right has three radio stations in town and another nearby in Portland. Around the clock those stations' hosts blast immigrants, blaming them for everything from the price of gas to terrorism. For years Ramon Ramirez, director of Oregon's largest Latino organization, Pineros y Campesinos Unidos de Noroeste (PCUN), has believed that a response, via radio, was called for. Finally PCUN got its own megaphone: a weekly show on a local commercial radio station. When Latino callers started phoning in with complaints about their working and living conditions, however, the commercial owners of the station hosting PCUN's show canceled it. "He said we were organizing," says Ramirez. "Well, sure enough, we never agreed to use our airtime to sell beer and push bad bands and encourage people to shop at Wal-Mart." So PCUN did what the Democrats have never done: they built their own radio station. Over a weekend in late summer PCUN and the Prometheus Radio project (a group that successfully sued the FCC to secure the right of low-power broadcasters to obtain legal licenses) invited hundreds of volunteers to participate in what they called a radio "barn-raising." Around three hundred showed up, working out of PCUN's union office in an old Methodist church surrounded by colorful murals to create the farmworkers' own station: KPCN. "There are simpler ways to start a radio station than have 250 people who've never turned a screwdriver before stick their hands in," says Peter Tridish of Prometheus. "But the birth of a station is a momentous occasion for social movements. Having everybody involved makes it clear that it's everybody's radio station."

Low-power FM is the farmworkers' equivalent of the blogosphere—not just a message device, it's a community builder. PCUN director Ramirez says he got a sense of the power of radio when he was working to organize strawberry pickers. He'd go out into the fields, and the air would be filled with the sound of scores of transistor radios tuned to the World Cup soccer tournament. "You can't take TV sets or computers into the fields," Ramirez explained soon after the KPCN "barn-raising." Old it may be, but radio's the perfect medium for people who need access to information that they dare not seek from official sources (their immigration status encourages extreme caution) or that they cannot find due to language barriers. KPCN will reach enough of the Woodburn area to cover the heart of the workers' community.

Ramirez plans to use the station to educate his members about how to use Oregon's mail-in voter system. He tells me about training programs he has in mind for women and youth. "We're also going to the radio as a way of educating ourselves about other communities, like the lesbian, gay, bisexual, and transgendered community," he told me, catching me by surprise, "so we can be better allies to that community."

John Kerry could have had a megaphone if he'd wanted one, and progressives do have media. Even before the mainstreaming of the Internet, we had a world of media. In contrast to the scene on the Right, ours was built up in spite of, not thanks to, forward-looking major donors. In 2000, in a rickety building across town from the Comcast First Union Center in Philadelphia, I had the pleasure of participating in a week of independent reporting on the Republican National Convention, followed by a second week of broadcasts from outside the Democratic National Convention in L.A. *Crashing the Party,* a nightly broadcast, went out live via the satellite channel Free Speech TV and was retransmitted via network, to about two hundred public-access cable stations, a few local PBS stations, and the Internet. Some twelve hundred independent journalists registered at the L.A. Independent Media Center for the convention. There were eight hundred in Philadelphia. *Crashing the Party* was an ambitious undertaking that brought together the talents of two or even three generations of progressive media activists and journalists. Everyone in the room worked for free. Each morning Amy Goodman would broadcast her crusading *Democracy Now* program to her community, to public radio affiliates, and simultaneously to the TV audience. Every evening I'd serve as a kind of video-deejay and host, juggling a cavalcade of expert guests, eyewitnesses to events, reporters, and entertainers, pieced together (sometimes not quite together) by independent media-makers with videocams and donated computers. In addition to the TV shows, a daily newspaper was published, and a twenty-four-hour radio station was created, with broadcasts for five days. Panel discussions were held outside on the street, taped, and broadcast. The topics were the ones the politicians and the parties were talking about—and the ones they weren't—brought live, in real time, to a television, radio, and print audience. While viewers were turning away from the ever-shrinking and largely stultifying coverage available on network TV, our independent broadcasts, produced on a pittance of what the networks spent, reached ten million households on DISH Network and eleven million homes on DirecTV. Forty-three community cable stations and community radio stations in cities across the United States broadcast the feed in real time. WYBE, Philly's smaller public television station, carried the programming and reported later that, based on the number of phone calls received (ten to one in our favor), more than 100,000 viewers tuned in each night to that station alone.

The people I saw each night were those who pioneered community access and coined the terms *indymedia, open source, listener-supported, eye-witness video,* and *free speech TV.* The reporters on the *Crashing the Party* broadcasts were veterans from left publications, the black press, the ethnic press, the queer media, the feminist media, independent film-makers, young reporters from Web- and radio-based youth media, and contributors to local Pacifica station KPFK. Among the performers were poets and cartoonists and recording artists, from Michael Franti to Jello Biafra, along with a whole slew of oddball comics in strange costumes.

Liberal donors like to say (and some have told me so directly) that they'd like to fund fresh media—they just don't know which ones. The reality is, *media* is a plural noun, an interactive ecology. Asking independent media to pick their "best" asset is like offering a barefoot man one boot for his "best" leg.

As the Right learned long ago, media have the most impact when they work collaboratively. With their think thanks, TV, radio, and print outlets working in consort, the Right created an echo chamber that amplified its core beliefs and made them sound mainstream (before they were). Not long ago, the publishers of *In These Times*, the *Nation, Mother Jones*, the *American Prospect*, and other progressive media came together to create something similar. They formed what became the Media Consortium, which had its first public outing in the fall of 2005. Consortium members scheduled articles to focus attention on Wal-Mart just as Robert Greenwald was releasing his film *Wal-Mart: The High Cost of Low Price*. Synergy has worked well for Greenwald, whose documentaries have found an audience without the help of the major distributors or network television. *Wal-Mart* was seen in living rooms, church halls, and pizza parlors, at screenings arranged and publicized by local independent media and activists, and the abusive practices of the world's largest supermarket chain became fodder for mainstream debate. "The thousands of individuals who distribute our DVDs are our Warner Brothers, our Loews," Greenwald told me. Don Hazen, executive editor at Alter-Net.org, one of the originators of the Consortium, is reservedly optimistic. "Independent media people are the very last people who want to sacrifice independence at the level of what we write, but new technology offers the possibility of new marriages of strategy and organizing."

New technologies also throw up new challenges for progressives and the Left. The Right enjoyed an advantage in that, in the 1970s and 1980s, when men like Buchanan and Weyrich mounted their assault on "mainstream media," there still was such a thing. Today the TV show that sparks a workplace water-cooler conversation has gone the way of the public-school lunch line or the public square. New media are growing in diversity and variety, but they—and their audiences—are increasingly fragmented. "How do we communicate with one another across racial, ethnic, class, and age boundaries on a horizontal axis that connects us, not just as blogger 'I's' but as entire communities?" asks Sandy Close, executive director and founder of New American Media.

The plethora of new media has given us way, way more to talk about, but shared conversation among people who are different seems to be going the way of the predigital radio dial. Most Americans still get their news from network TV (and a single newspaper, *USA Today*), but that proportion has been shrinking and splintering as people abandon the network news for the Internet, independent media, and "niche-marketed" media aimed at sports fans, history buffs, music fans, and all manner of ethnic groups. Political partisans can survive on a diet of the news and opinion they like best; nothing else need interrupt their universe. Much as I love my listeners on Air America Radio, for example, it worries me how little they like to hear from anyone with an opposing view. It's a knee-jerk reaction: whenever I entertain a call from a conservative, the phone lines light up and my e-mail box fills with listeners furious that I've fallen prey to a right-wing plot. "Dittoheads have their own airwaves," one listener wrote. That seems to me to be the problem.

Finally, new or old, when it comes to making change, the media are only as good as the messages they carry. Progressive media exist; it's the movements the progressives lack.

The last weekend in August 2005, *RadioNation* broadcast live from Crawford, Texas. It's hard to imagine how Cindy Sheehan's antiwar vigil at the gates of the president's ranch could have grown into a hundreds-strong presence without consistent coverage in the independent media. Daily, even hourly, reports on Air America Radio and on community radio inspired members of military families and others to pack into their cars and join Sheehan's vigil. They'd call *RadioNation* as they headed south. Numbers swelled for days before the press corps even mentioned the protest, and more than a week passed before one journalist at last asked the president Sheehan's question: What is the just cause in Iraq? On my way home from Texas, I watched the Weather Channel on the airport monitors, warning of what looked like a barometric Armageddon heading toward the Gulf Coast of Mississippi, Alabama, and Louisiana. That night, and for days afterward, I talked with a few lonely souls who'd stayed behind in New Orleans, among them Malik Rahim, who reported, breathless from hauling water for his neighbors from blocks away, or slightly nervous, describing the mobs of young white men and freelance "security" contractors who were cruising around his neighborhood, their automatic weapons pointed his way. Independent media helped Rahim's cause too—but not enough.

Some very skeptical executives at Air America Radio agreed to let me pack my radio equipment into a small rolling bag and meet this Rahim for myself. The streetlights weren't working and large parts of New Orleans still had no water. We ended up broadcasting live from the headquarters of Rahim's organization, Common Ground Relief, in the unflooded neighborhood of Algiers. We broadcast from the kitchen table of Malik and his wife, Sharon, in fact. (At one point their rooster, Roo, flew onto the set and squawked his views.) In those days, small groups like Common Ground were the only ones operating in the worst-hit parts of town. Volunteers and a tiny handful of local residents struggled to haul trash, empty abandoned refrigerators, feed people, find water, and protect local homes from bulldozers. The sole evidence of government at work was the police cars that cruised by, sometimes littering or worse, as they passed. It was hard to keep the fury out of my voice as I broadcast from a buckling table surrounded by low- or no-income people, who, abandoned by the state, were attempting to take on the state's work.

A year later (this time with producer Christabel Nsiah-Buadi), *RadioNation* returned to New Orleans. While we were there, the president made a lightning-fast appearance and ate crawfish with Mayor

Ray Nagin. George Bush went to Jackson Square and said he could not imagine America without the Crescent City and pledged that "our" government would do its part. Eleven months after Katrina hit, as far as I could see, "our" government wasn't doing much of anything but giving away taxpayer dollars to Bush's contractor colleagues. On the one-year anniversary of the breaking of the levees in New Orleans, a third of the city *still* had no electricity. More than half of the population still hadn't come home. In the poorest and blackest parts of town, individual people were still hauling trash, disposing of decomposed meat, feeding their neighbors, and foraging for water and fuel. In the hardest-hit parts of the city, volunteers were still the only ones reclaiming anybody's homes. And they were still alone. And they were still finding dead bodies.

It's not as if the story had been hidden. In the weeks after Katrina hit, CNN's Anderson Cooper and NBC's Brian Williams more or less made New Orleans their beat. Hordes of reporters flew in and out; thousands of volunteers from church groups, high schools, and colleges came, some on spring break, to work, and to see for themselves. Nonprofits from Oxfam to the Sierra Club sent in everyone from sociologists to soil scientists and published no end of reports. Wynton Marsalis and Aaron Neville gathered the crème de la crème of the music world to raise money for the Big Easy's artists. Spike Lee produced a well-received and massively publicized HBO movie, and MoveOn organized members into meet-ups to watch it.

The problem was not the lack of a megaphone. A year of reporting, blogging, and talking had held up a powerful megaphone to what was left of the Gulf Coast. The problem was the lack of an effective government—or popular response. In the silence where policy proposals should have been, there were appeals but no action at the federal, state, or local level. Nor were there effective demonstrations in the nation's streets. It took the satirical political performance group the Yes Men to say what public housing officials should have said: open up all public housing units. (Instead the New Orleans Housing Authority declared that even unflooded units would be destroyed.) It was a member of ACORN who asked the city council what happened to rent control. (After the hurricane, average rents in New Orleans soared from about $600 a month to twice that for a small apartment.) On *RadioNation* Eloise Williams, a grandmother living with her five traumatized grandchildren (including eight-year-old Joneisha, who saw dead bodies float by her in the floodwater), asked simply, why not extend Medicare to everyone and include mental health coverage? Instead of setting arbitrary deadlines and penalties for property clean-up, what about issuing tickets for displaced survivors to come back and inspect their property? Malcolm Suber of the People's Hurricane Relief Fund pointed out that Iraqi refugees in Detroit had been helped to vote in their country's election; why not make that same method of voting available to Louisiana's displaced around the nation?

The Right's media project was effective because it worked hand in hand with movements that had clear policy priorities. The neoconservatives' aim was to shift the burden of responsibility for the poor and the weak from the state and the taxpayer onto the poor and the weak themselves. Their reality-shifting project has worked to such an extent that even a disaster that displaced two million Americans, destroyed 350,000 homes, and revealed the chasm that is left of our social safety net was not enough to trigger a substantive debate about the causes of poverty and the role of government in alleviating it. New Orleans mayor Ray Nagin told the people he works for and the people who elected him, the city's residents, that they could return to their city, but "at your own risk." No one flinched. Our shrinking expectations of politicians and politics itself are the result of a long-term right-wing project. It demands a long-term response that no end of media can produce without a movement that sets it as its priority.

With all due respect to Marshall McLuhan, the medium is not the message. Not in the sense that new technology necessarily opens up new debate. Over the span of thirty years, a concerted conservative movement has used its media not just to win power in government, but to transform government itself and overhaul the public's expectations about the relationship between citizens and the state. As a new century starts, progressive media don't match the conservatives' arsenal just yet, but enough progressive media exist to make an impact. We have the media; it's the movements we lack—movements powerful enough to force a national reassessment.

CHAPTER EIGHT ☆ Mobbing Up

"I don't want everybody to vote. Elections are not won by a majority of the people. They never have been from the beginning of our country and they are not now. As a matter of fact, our leverage in the elections quite candidly goes up as the voting populace goes down."

—New Right strategist PAUL WEYRICH,
at a training session for fifteen thousand
conservative preachers in Dallas, 1979[1]

"In America, it is vital that every vote count, and that every vote be counted. But . . ."

—JOHN KERRY, concession speech,
Boston, November 3, 2004

As I drove east from Louisiana, I thought I'd left the land of broken levees, but when I turned off the interstate and dropped down into Northwest Miami, I found myself in a similar place again, looking at blocks of rubble and boarded-up public housing projects. Abandoned baby carriages jutted up-ended into rotting garbage; children's scooters rusted in the mud. Later I had a hard time identifying the pictures I took of the urban wasteland that was once public housing in Florida; they looked so much like pictures of the Ninth Ward in New Orleans.

Primary day falls during hurricane season in Miami. The rain is heavy, the turnout light. When I showed up in September 2006, a bevy of displaced public housing residents were distributing campaign leaflets to voters, and more were working inside the precincts. Rain or no rain, they were glad to have the work. According to the latest census, 19 percent of the people in Miami-Dade County live below the federal poverty line (of $20,000 for a family of four), but around here the percentage is higher than that. Condominium towers are rising downtown, and business is booming for property speculators, but for renters Miami has become the most unaffordable city in the country. Six years ago the local housing authority moved some six thousand people out of two projects here, on a promise that demolition and affordable new homes would follow, but just three such homes have been built; the rest of the place is flattened, and most of the development money has been spent. As Mary Nesbitt, who lived twenty-eight years in the projects, told me, "We had our Katrina here, but ours came in walking, not blowing."

A day's pay is a day's pay. Under the circumstances I expected the poll workers to be cynical about the actual voting. Besides, this is Miami-Dade, home of the great vote-suppression exercise that brought us President George W. Bush in 2000. If Manhattan is ground zero for the wartime president, Miami-Dade is Cape Canaveral for Bush's presidency. Here Haitian immigrants were denied bilingual ballots; here voters were asked for multiple IDs; and here, when a recount was finally ordered to make sense of all the hanging chads, a small group of thugs with ties to the Republican Party was able to invade the county executive's office and shut down the counting with a lot of shouting and waving of fists. Given all that, I wouldn't have been surprised if no one working the polls gave a toss about elections or voting. But I was wrong. The more we talked, the clearer it became that these $87-a-day poll-working poor-folk may well be our democracy's first line of defense.

Taking refuge from the rain on some evicted person's porch, Malcolm R. points out a slow-moving ninety-four-year-old woman he's seen vote every election since he's given such things a thought. "She cares about the voting because voting's all we got," Malcolm tells me, nipping out from the shelter of the porch to hand her a leaflet. "Plus voting's a right our people fought for." At fifty-five, Malcolm says he's never missed an election himself, except once when he was in Vietnam.

"In 2000 I worked the polls and I saw what happened," says a woman who explains that she's living in a shelter these days and goes by the name Corinne. "Long lines, people turned away, men that shouted, machines that broke. It wasn't right."

From her seat on a very wet bedroom cabinet (now on the porch) Moselle Rackard, a former saleswoman, pipes up. "If Democrats were in power, things would be different. Democrats put things in order. They put people to work. Even now Democrats are working to help poor people. Republicans only help themselves. That's why I vote for Democrats."

It's sobering to sit on someone's evicted, rain-soaked furniture and listen to poor people talk about the preciousness of elections and why they vote for Democrats.

In *What's the Matter with Kansas?*, Thomas Frank claimed that poor voters in Kansas had been hoodwinked by the Right and distracted from their self-interest over issues having to do with gays and guns and God. The argument resonated with liberals who have been befuddled by the defeat of their favorite candidates, but there were some problems with Frank's book. Its central thesis, to start. As Princeton politics professor Larry Bartels revealed, Frank's case holds up only if the working class is defined by educational attainment. Defined by income, the white working class hasn't abandoned Democrats. Low-income white southerners defected with the Dixiecrats to the GOP over racial equality and civil rights, but the only income group that's been abandoning the Democrats is the rich. CNN exit polls revealed that 55 percent of under-$50,000 earners voted Democratic; only 35 percent of those earning more than $200,000 did. Bush's largest margin of victory came among those earning $200,000 or more. Kerry's came among those earning $15,000 or less. (Kerry won 63 percent of those votes.)

Half of all Americans earn less than $30,000 a year. They vote blue. As do people of color: in 2004 African Americans voted 88 percent blue; Latinos 56 percent. In late October 2006, George Bush's support among African Americans had dropped to just 2 percent.

Demographic trends predict that the United States will be a "majority minority" country by 2050. Given that reality, the future for Democrats should look bright. There's just one glitch: the rich outvote the poor. In 2004, according to the census, 81.3 percent of those who earned $100,000 or more cast a ballot, while only 48 percent of those who earned less than $20,000 voted. The poorer you are in America, the less likely you are to vote. The reasons are manifold: nothing to vote for, no candidate who cares, long lines, no time, no up-to-date voter registration, fear. Another factor is the absence in America of an assumption of "innocence" while voting. In contrast to most advanced democracies, the right to vote in the United States isn't conveyed automatically with citizenship and coming of age. Voters have to prove themselves and always have, and the challenges related to registering, qualifying, and having one's vote be counted have always worked to help manipulate or suppress votes.

The U.S. Constitution guarantees no affirmative, fundamental right to vote. To quote Representative Jesse L. Jackson Jr. (Democrat of Illinois), "Voting in America is overseen by 13,000 different election administrations, all separate and unequal." Instead, voting is governed by local authorities in fifty states who oversee 4,600 different systems; it is implemented by 22,000 officials, with 700,000 voting machines, and 1.4 million minimally trained poll workers. Rules and regulations vary not only from state to state but from county to county. From felon disenfranchisement laws to monolingual ballots and myriad, ever-changing requirements for registration and identification, the hurdles to voting are legion and rising. In the 1800s it was the working class and Irish immigrants who were hurt by special registration rules in cities, and by sunset laws that closed polling places before factory workers got out of work. Today it is young people, people who relocate frequently, African Americans, immigrants, and non–English speakers who have the hardest time registering and casting a vote. The voters upon whom a Democratic majority depends are the very ones whose rights have been the hardest to secure and the easiest to violate. Currently their grip on the franchise is still fragile at best. The system invites abuse, and it's anything but nonpartisan. In thirty-three states the top election cop is neither an independent official nor a public commission but an elected partisan. In Ohio in 2004 that person was Secretary of State Kenneth Blackwell, who was also cochair of the state Bush/Cheney re-election campaign. In Florida in 2000 it was Katherine Harris, simulta-neously the state's top election cop and cochair of the committee to elect Bush/Cheney.

Gihan Perera remembers receiving calls in 2000 from poll workers telling him that boxes of what looked like ballots were still lying around at some precincts. Perera directs the Miami Workers Center, to which many of the poll workers I met belong. In 2000 one member, who served as a poll worker, found a box marked "Miami Dade Ballots" in a church days after it should have been collected. Five days into the vote-count controversy, another worker found a full ballot box on a shelf in a nursing home. Perera is no election expert. He's a union organizer from the San Francisco Bay Area whose parents came to the United States from Sri Lanka. The Workers Center is a poor-people's organization squeezed into an old bank, next to the neighborhood barbershop. Perera remembers thinking, "C'mon, we don't count on the Democratic Party for much, but aren't these your elections, your candidates, your votes, your voters. . . . Isn't this your job?"

As the 2002 Florida gubernatorial race approached, Perera and his colleagues looked with trepidation for some sign of life across the street. A big placard on the other side of Northwest Seventh Avenue declared: "Miami-Dade Democratic Party (North District)." Below it is an "I Have a Dream" mural bearing Dr. Martin Luther King Jr.'s face. "After what happened in 2000, we sat like Katrina victims on their rooftops waiting for the helicopters to come and rescue us," said Perera. "Then we realized no one was coming." Over at the North Miami-Dade Democratic Party office nothing stirred.

In the fall of 2004 the Democratic Party in most states was like the one in that office on Northwest Seventh Avenue: nice mural, nobody home. As it turns out, the North Miami-Dade office had moved away and never taken down the sign, but local party offices typically function for only as long as there's money and volunteers, usually ten or twelve weeks leading up to an election, then shut up tight.

Immediately after the 2004 election a nonprofit group called Grassroots Democrats surveyed forty state parties and found that 62 percent had no full-time communications director—which is to say no one to communicate to voters, the media, legislators, or state officials, let alone anyone to meet with grassroots organizers between elections. Grassroots Democrats director Amy Chapman, who's worked in party politics for years, thought she knew how dire things were: "I'd heard about lack of permanency, staffers and leaders leaving after an election. . . . People being laid-off right after the vote because the party can't pay their salary. That's normal." But she was taken aback to find that in many places even compliance officers had to be let go—before they'd filled out the year-end reports. That's tantamount to putting a sticker on your head that reads "Audit me."

In 2004 some organizers made waves simply by pledging "We'll be here the morning after." That's what the League of Pissed-Off Voters promised people in Ohio. The presidential election results ended up hinging on some very questionable numbers from that state, a place where some voters spent hours standing in line in the rain; reports of voter-suppression were rampant. At that point the League's Amy Kaplan told my radio show that having amped up the hopes of so many, "we just couldn't walk away." Bob Fitrakis, a local political scientist and the editor of Ohio's independent journal FreePress.org, had served as an international election monitor; what he saw in Columbus on Election Day sounded alarm bells in his head. When he heard Kerry and Edwards concede, he remembered the older black gentleman who'd been ahead of him in the voting line, quietly singing "Ain't gonna turn me 'round, turn me 'round. . . ." It made Fitrakis angry. "They're not going to stand up for voters who stood for seven hours for them? What's wrong with these people?" With no help from the Democratic Party, the Kerry campaign, or the 527s that had already left Ohio on November 13, Fitrakis, Kaplan, and the Citizens' Alliance for Secure Elections held public hearings to investigate and document what voters had experienced. Hundreds of witnesses trekked in from all across the state and testified that voters in African American and overwhelmingly Democratic areas had waited for hours, while voters in affluent suburbs were in and out in minutes, with no ID checks, no shortage of voting machines, and no voter challenges. One witness, Tanikka Henriquez, age twenty-nine, had waited over four hours in the voting line in inner-city Columbus; she said the experience reminded her of what she'd heard about Jim Crow. Poll workers and precinct judges testified that some precincts had fewer election machines in operation on November 2 than they had had for the less-well-attended 2004 primary. "After that a lot of people felt, see, this is why we don't vote," said Henriquez.

Making a commitment to voters that they'll "be there the morning after" is not something that electoral campaigns do. They're out to win the election, period. It's the party that has the treasury. Senate and congressional campaign committees interview candidates and decide whom to back for Senate and House races. Candidates race, and campaigns campaign. The Democratic National Committee's job is to build a national majority that can elect a president. DNC chairs normally do that from Washington, deciding where to send money and troops at the last minute; it could also be done from the states. Over the last many years party leaders have adopted the former course. Investors want to back winners, not long shots; with limited resources campaign staff are not interested in "being there" the morning after. They're there to win and that's it. In 2004 the number of truly contested states shrank to seventeen out of fifty, then seven. Swing states saw an infusion of money and people and a barrage of TV ads—but states that weren't "swinging" saw very little—not money, not candidates, not campaign leaflets.

When the Democratic Party controlled either the Congress or the White House, "we were comfortable," Donna Brazile told me. Brazile served as Al Gore's campaign manager in 2000. Party leaders had enough power and ability-to-deliver that they could inject money where it was needed to hire temporary workers to win an election even without a vibrant state-level infrastructure. Political action committees (PACs) raised money; nonprofit advocates communicated issues; and nonpartisan get-out-the-vote efforts received contracts based on a calculation of dollars-per-ballot delivered. "We thought as long as we were a majority and we had an honest chance, every two or four years, of winning back the majority, we didn't have to invest the kind of resources into technology and fifty state organizations," continued Brazile. "When Republicans began to win races at the state and local level and claimed the Great Plains states, the heartland, and the South, Democrats retreated," she continued. "They just absolutely retreated."

But the road to free and fair elections is long. The federal government establishes standards, but policies on registration and voter ID and the distribution of polling machines are set by counties and state officials months, sometimes years, in advance. By the time campaign activists arrive, the damage, if damage there be, has been done. Relying on getting an "honest chance" every two or four years with new draftees is tantamount to entering a war zone blindfolded, with not one but two hands tied behind you, fingers crossed.

In Ohio former Clinton aide Harold Ickes told reporters the day after the 2004 election that America Coming Together, which had spearheaded the get-out-the-vote effort, had "hit all its goals" and that he didn't believe that investigating "voting irregularities" would change who was going to occupy the White House. In his concession speech John Kerry uttered these revealing words: "In America, it is vital that every vote count, and that every vote be counted. But..." That was it. He conceded, and like Gore before him, once he conceded, he didn't want to look back. "In 2000 we left the battlefield," says Brazile. "We didn't even want to go on the battlefield.... After 2004 I cussed them out, because I was begging for money to conduct an investigation."

Howard Dean, in his most famous picture, has his sleeves rolled up, his fist in the air, his face flushed, and his mouth open. It's not a bad image for the man who wants to take the Democratic Party back into the fight. "After the election I felt that this country needed change desperately and the Democratic Party was in terrible trouble," Dean told me in a conversation from his office a month before the 2006 elections.

He considered building a third party out of the PAC his campaign had spawned, Democracy for America, now headed by his brother Jim. But a third party, Dean says he concluded, "just wasn't statistically very likely to have any impact," at least not in the short term, and the former Vermont governor is an impatient man, a doctor who knows the perils of waiting for treatment. Dean concluded that the nation couldn't afford to wait. "Bush was doing so much damage to the country, we needed to stop him."

What Dean has going for him is that he's not a self-made man. On the campaign trail he learned that when he opened his mouth, people responded, especially when he said clear-sounding things like "end the war in Iraq." People at the grass roots, parched for any candidate with an ounce of passion, turned a conservative Vermont governor into a progressive by flooding his campaign with their ideas and their cash. Dean's campaign received more money over the Internet than any campaign ever had, and his primary race surfaced Democratic voters who hadn't been active for years, at least not for a Democrat. Contrary to the firebrand image he acquired in the media, Dean himself is no firebrand ideologically. He admits that he simply went with the flow and, along the way, acquired a belief in the value of opening up a space and seeing who showed up to fill it.

"The most important innovation is this: we learned to take ideas from the bottom—the grass roots—and to call on them for our ideas and actions during the campaign. We had a conversation going with our supporters. That wasn't tried in the Kerry campaign," Dean told the progressive website Alternet.org soon after the 2004 election.

After the 2004 primary season produced Kerry rather than Dean as the Democratic candidate, Dean's supporters didn't fade away. They created blogs, formed meet-up groups, and contributed to Democracy for America. Some founded an "inside-outside" pressure group that held its founding convention in New Jersey in the summer of 2004, calling itself Progressive Democrats of America (PDA). As word got out that Dean was considering his options for what to do next, Tim Carpenter, executive director of PDA, says, "We drafted Dean" to run as chairman of the Democratic National Committee (DNC). The DNC is the membership organization of party leaders and statewide committee people. Dean ran for the chairmanship and famously called every member, but so did Carpenter's people, most of whom were party activists, some with long records organizing in the states. When Dean won, Carpenter says, the stage was set for a "collision" between the establishment party, with its money in the suites and paid freelancers in the streets, and what he calls the grassroots party, or those others who had been working for Kerry, Gore, and Clinton for the lack of anyone else.

"The Return of the Angry Man," ran the headline over a profile of Dean in the *Washington Post.* That adjective has dogged Dean ever since the night that red-faced picture was snapped, on January 19, 2004, the night his primary bid went down to an embarrassing third-place defeat in the Iowa caucuses. Caught on a mike that stripped out all the surrounding sound and turned his voice into what became "the Scream," one part of that night's speech was piteously repeated: "Not only are we going to New Hampshire . . . we're going to South Carolina and Oklahoma and Arizona and North Dakota and New Mexico, and we're going to California and Texas and New York. . . . And we're going to South Dakota and Oregon and Washington and Michigan. And then we're going to Washington, D.C., to take back the White House! Yaaah!!!"

As it turns out, Dean's been giving pretty much the same speech ever since becoming DNC chair (although more quietly). In 2004 he thundered encouragement to raise the spirits of a downcast staff in Iowa. Since then, he's become cheerleader chairman of a downcast Democratic Party.

Progressives like Tim Carpenter hope that Dean, as head of the DNC, will open up that conversation all across the country. In the first four months of his chairmanship, Dean visited twenty-three states, ten of them Republican, or "red." What he found were state Democratic Party chairs furious about being sidelined and races that were going uncontested even at the county and district level, where winning a seat is cheap. Even some of the state parties that had been targeted, battleground states were in disarray. (When Dean came on board, the IRS had a lien on the assets of the Florida state party to the tune of some $200,000 for failure to pay Social Security taxes and disability insurance on its employees.) If even some of the better-endowed states were stumbling, the nonbattleground states were like graveyards, and nowhere was the situation worse than in the Deep South. In 2004 the Mississippi Democratic Party had just one full-time staff person. Keelan Sanders served eighty-two counties with twenty-five hundred precincts. His title was spiffy—executive director—but he had no staff and no one to direct.

"The easy solution, which has been employed for the last twenty-five years, is to focus on the next election ahead of you," Dean explained. "In which case at the end of every two-year cycle we're broke and there's no innovation because there's no money to do innovation and there's no serious attention to how to fix anything because everything is an emergency." Perhaps Dean has picked up some ideas from his feminist wife, Judy Steinberg, such as, "the personal is political." He certainly seems to believe that the way the party treats its own sends a message. "I believe it's contagious," says Dean. "Being in all fifty states to give our message shows people who aren't respectful of Democrats that we respect ourselves, and I believe that's contagious and they'll respect us."

In 2005, breaking with the penthouse party way of doing things, Dean unrolled what he called his Fifty-State Strategy. Rather than allocate maximum resources to a minimum number of high-stakes races, Dean's DNC started placing people in all fifty states—paid nationally, hired locally—to fill positions even in places where the party hadn't been competitive in decades—like Mississippi. The DNC put up the money for a new-voter file, at a cost of $8 million; as of September 2006 about forty-five states were using it, and about two hundred field staff had been hired and trained, between two and four in every state. Howard Dean and those charged with electing Democrats to Congress and the Senate were on a collision course over the use of resources, but relationships between the national party and the state parties were looking up.

I arrived in Jackson on August 30, 2006. Opening the door of the Mississippi Democratic Party office was Rita Royals, a fifty-seven-year-old white woman and former rape crisis counselor who became so frustrated with the sleepy state of her local party that a few years back she pulled together her own independent club of prochoice, antiwar progressives ("sixty-five of my friends who weren't afraid to say they were Democrats").

"When I first came through the door," Royals tells me, she looked around, saw Keelan Sanders all alone in the office, and wondered where everybody else was. In 2004 the DNC invested so little in this state that Royals paid out of her own pocket to print John Kerry signs. Today she is back on a crisis hotline of sorts. One of Dean's new hires, she spends her days calling Democratic county chairs who haven't heard from anyone from the head office in years, let alone someone who is asking them to get to work. Royals shares an office with co–field director DeMiktric Biggs, who has been attending party committee meetings since he was in his sophomore year. "They didn't really want me," he says, "but I kept turning up." The DNC's stated goal was for every precinct in every state to have a precinct captain by the 2006 midterm vote. To that end, Royals and Biggs were asking the chairs to take responsibility for finding captains for every precinct in their county. Some respond really well, some less so, says Biggs. It depends how they like being stirred up. The biggest surprise Royals and Biggs have come across so far is the age of the people they're calling. Most are over fifty, one is eighty years old, and most have held the same post for a dozen years. "Some way more than that," says Biggs. When we meet in August, Biggs and Royals believe they're on track. They've called every chair. "They haven't all called us back, but we've called," says Royals, smiling.

A special mayoral election was coming up in the Delta town of Greenwood, so the state party staff set off to pay a visit. The remarkable thing about this visit was not only that the journey was made at all but that making it required two cars. Along with Sanders came Biggs and Jay Parmley, former chair of the Oklahoma party and a key southern ally of Dean's. Parmley had initially opposed Dean, then changed his mind. "He understood that much more was possible out here than we were given credit for, but we were stranded." Parmley is on loan from the DNC to the Mississippi party for a year. Also on the Greenwood trip were Wayne Dowdy, the state party chairman, and Wendi Hooks, the finance director. As soon as they arrived in mayoral candidate Sheriel Perkins's office, Dowdy, a patrician former congressman, put both hands palms down on the conference table, looked her in the eye, and said, "You are our first priority."

It was no insignificant gesture. Perkins was facing a special election in the Greenwood mayoral race because a judge had declared that the mayoral race of a year earlier had been skewed by fraud. When Sheriel, a three-term city councilwoman, and her husband, Willie, a state rep, went to bed on that election night, election officials had certified the count, putting her ahead by two hundred votes. When they woke up, enough absentee ballots had appeared to return the twelve-year incumbent to office by a margin of just six votes. Suspecting fraud but not attributing blame to anyone in particular, the judge called for a new election. Perkins stood to become the first woman mayor of Greenwood and the first African American mayor in that historic town in the heart of Mississippi's plantation flatlands. A river town just upstream from Jackson, Greenwood was once the cotton capital of the world; it had been the capital, too, of white supremacy, or at least of the White Citizens Council in these parts. When Dr. Martin Luther King Jr. touched down here in 1964 to show his support for Freedom Summer and the work of the civil rights movement, it was a speedy trip, and an FBI escort accompanied him all the way through town. A hundred eleven prisoners (including Stokely Carmichael, who is said to have coined the term "Black Power" in Greenwood) were just then emerging from jail, after a six-day hunger strike, incarcerated for the innocent crime of being black and standing in line at the courthouse to register, holding "One Man/One Vote" picket signs.

The one man (and one woman)/one vote struggle is not over. In fact, the picket signs have been making a comeback. During the vote-count fiasco in Florida, they were out on the sidewalk in front of the Miami-Dade County executive's office. In Ohio they showed up at the public hearings in Columbus. During the five years following the signing of the Voting Rights Act in August 1965, as many southern blacks were registered as had been registered in the previous one hundred years. The number of African American elected officials in the South jumped accordingly, from seventy-two in 1965 to almost five thousand by 1993. As the number of minority, Democratically inclined voters has grown and with them every manner of registration effort, some Republicans are trying to win elections by suppressing the vote of those who are likely to vote against them. And the Democratic Party is just waking up to this reality.

Fighting fraud is the passion of both the Bush Justice Department and its allies in the states, even though even they can produce precious little evidence of fraud occurring. The "new face of Jim Crow," as Elliot Mincberg of People for the American Way describes it, is voter suppression in the name of fighting fraud: on top of felon disenfranchisement, we're talking about photo ID requirements, restrictions on voter-registration efforts, and the denial of bilingual ballots under "English-only" laws. In Ohio a statewide survey found four instances of ineligible people voting or attempting to vote in 2002 and 2004 out of close to ten million votes cast. A survey in Washington state following the 2004 election found fewer than one case per 100,000 ballots.

The most-often-occurring form of fraud is the sort that cropped up in the Greenwood mayoral race involving mailed-in absentee ballots. Voter-identification laws don't stop that. Nonetheless, states around the nation have passed stringent ID rules. While it's not unreasonable to request some proof of identity when voters register, Georgia passed a rule that required voters who didn't have a driver's license to buy a voter ID card. When the law went into effect, there was no office in the entire city of Atlanta that sold the card. A federal judge finally struck the rule down, calling it a virtual poll tax on the 300,000 people who needed the card—disproportionately old people and African Americans.

In 2000 the state of Florida purged thousands of sometimes entirely legitimate voters' names from the voting rolls in advance of the 2000 election. Many states, including Ohio, conducted massive purges in advance of 2004. In 2006 a judge had to intervene to stop a flawed last-minute purge in Kentucky. After local groups conducted massive voter-registration drives, states including Missouri and Florida adopted such strict rules for voter registration that the League of Women Voters of Florida, for the first time in its history, stopped registering people to vote, for fear of incurring weighty criminal and civil penalties. And then there is the question of unverified, and in some cases unverifiable, electronic voting machines.

After the disaster of the 2000 election, Congress passed the Help

America Vote Act of 2002 (HAVA), which required states to replace their old lever voting machines and "hanging-chad" ballots with new, supposedly accessible machines. But in and of themselves the new machines have created a whole new world of problems, from simple malfunctions (backing up voting lines) to lost votes, lost machines, and proprietary software that the machine makers won't submit to independent scrutiny.

While local authorities, who set election rules, were devising new gauntlets for some voters to run, at the federal level the Bush administration brought with it into power some of the conservative movement's most seasoned vote suppressors. (They call themselves fighters of fraud.) Under the Voting Rights Act (which was reluctantly reauthorized by southern Republicans in the summer of 2006), the Civil Rights Division of the Justice Department is supposed to review states' election laws with a view to preventing them from having any negative impact on minorities, specifically African Americans. Under Bush the person in charge of that division was a former Federalist Society lawyer and former county Republican Party chair from Georgia, Hans von Spakovsky. In Georgia, Von Spakovsky fought for mandatory photo IDs for voters, even after experts ran the numbers and found that the rate of driver's license possession among African Americans was half of that for whites.

In 1997 Hans von Spakovsky prepared a paper that called for the massive "purging" of felons from voter rolls to "combat fraud." Von Spakovsky spent the thirty-six days of the Florida recount as a volunteer for Bush/Cheney. After the inauguration, the Voting Section of the Civil Rights Division hired him to oversee negotiations over the Help America Vote Act (2002). In a recess appointment in December 2005 the president named him to the board of the Federal Election Commission, the agency that was just then gearing up for the reauthorization of the forty-year-old Voting Rights Act.

If it weren't for a network of outside-the-party activists, the problems facing voters might never have made it onto the Democratic Party's radar. "Maybe you don't hear about the bad things happening when you win," Ted Kalo, minority general counsel for John Conyers of the House Judiciary Committee, told me. "Maybe they're happening, but you get the result that you want, so you kind of pay it no mind and move on." For many of the eight years Bill Clinton was in the White House, Brenda Wright was a lawyer in the Voting Rights Division. "The things that are happening now just weren't on the radar screen then," she told me.

Our electoral system is facing a perfect storm of a bad election law and bad economics, and the impact is being felt most acutely in blue spots on the map. Democratic voters are concentrated in urban areas whose infrastructures have been hollowed out by decades of privatization, disinvestment, deregulation, and the contracting power of social services and local government. If problems occur, most will occur where the most people live and where conditions are worst. In 2000 it was Miami (certain parts), in 2004 Columbus and New Orleans, and elections have gone awry in scores of places since. In a special election in California's fiftieth district in 2006, a Republican was declared the winner even after massive irregularities, including poll workers taking machines home with them overnight. In primaries in Maryland voters were turned away after precinct workers were unable to turn the machines on. Computers misidentified some people's party affiliations, and machines disappeared, turning up days later with the untallied votes still on them. It took ten days to count the provision ballots. Those votes that were recorded only electronically left no paper trail for a recount.

Because the Democratic Party has left voter-registration and get-out-the-vote operations to outsiders, it's no wonder those "outsiders" have been first to see—and fight—abuse.

In Miami the Miami Workers Center and the Miami-Dade Coalition for Election Reform have mobilized local groups to defend the right to vote. In 2002 the coalition pressured county commissioners to pass a resolution instructing the Miami-Dade County elections department to grant independent monitors access to the precincts. Commissioners, even liberal Democrats, were aghast, but the activists brought in enough poll workers, disenfranchised voters, and elections experts to sway public opinion. In 2002, for the first time in U.S. history, an election was monitored by international observers: the Florida gubernatorial race in Miami-Dade.

At the level of voter registration, Democracia USA, a Florida-based project of the People for the American Way Foundation, registered 72,000 mostly new Hispanic voters in 2004. In early 2006, their work came under threat from a sweeping new law passed by the state legislature. The law threatened to impose crippling fines on groups whose registrars submitted even a single flawed form. Frightened, some nonprofits called off their registration efforts for months. Lawyers from the Miami-Dade Coalition successfully sued and got the law reversed. The suspension of the law came just weeks before the midterm vote—but it was a victory for citizen voter-registrars. "We're not going to be bullied and we're going to fight," Coalition lawyer Lida Rodriguez-Taseff told *RadioNation* when we broadcast from Miami on Labor Day weekend.

In the absence of party leadership, a national vote-protection movement has forced the issue of disenfranchisement and electronic voting into the media and into the public consciousness. In the run-up to the congressional elections of 2006 those local activists linked up into national networks led by civil rights organizations and the electronic voting reform coalition VoteTrustUSA. They set up voter hotlines and deployed thousands of lawyers; others even organized volunteer crews to videotape goings-on at the precincts. At the end of the day, Common

Cause reported receiving 16,000 calls to its hotline. The Lawyers' Committee for Civil Rights Under Law handled 20,000. People for the American Way's vote-theft hotline received 21,000 calls from forty-five states, according to Stacey Gates, a spokeswoman. In terms of a dress rehearsal for 2008, the congressional midterms succeeded in showing up all the glitches voting-protection activists and their lawyers had been predicting: hours-long lines at polling places (this time in Colorado), badly functioning equipment, poorly trained poll workers, harassing "robocalls," and Jim Crow tactics in abundance. In Democrat Loretta Sanchez's California district, 14,000 letters were sent out to people with Hispanic last names warning immigrants that they could be deported if they voted. The letters were traced to a campaign worker in her opponent's office. Julia Carson, the first African American congresswoman from the Indianapolis district in Indiana was told by adamant poll workers that her congressional ID was unacceptable. The same thing happened to the secretary of state of Missouri: despite the Missouri Supreme Court's having overturned the state's photo ID law as unconstitutional, a poll worker tried to force Missouri secretary of state Robin Carnahan to show hers before she was allowed to vote.

At the end of the night, the fate of the Senate rested on tightly contested races in Montana, where voting machines in some precincts were held up by a software failure, and Virginia, where a margin of less than 0.5 percent of the vote triggered an automatic recount. Control of the Senate was determined by votes cast on optical scanning machines with no paper record, making a recount impossible.

With Democrats in power in Congress, elections activists are calling for change. Legislation sponsored by Representative Rush Holt (Democrat of New Jersey) would mandate paper trails on electronic machines. Representative Jesse L. Jackson Jr. (Democrat of Illinois) has sponsored a bill that calls for a Constitutional amendment to establish

MOBBING UP ☆ 203

a federal right to vote. Senator Barack Obama (Democrat of Illinois) has a bill that would impose harsh penalties for intimidating and deceptive practices. Up to now, the Democratic Party leadership has lagged behind its own voters.

"I can't tell you how hard official Washington of both parties has worked (for the most part) to avoid even considering that election machines don't work. I don't know why. It seems like all official Washington seemed to have a psychological investment in not wanting to take on this issue," Howard Dean told me.

The DNC's Voting Rights Institute, started by Donna Brazile after the 2000 debacle, has limped along with little support. (Brazile told me she had to appeal to the full membership to fund it at all. "I didn't trust I'd get a penny from the leadership.") In 2006 the DNC set up its own 1-888-DEM-VOTE hotline, but neither Dean nor Brazile nor the institute's director, Greg Moore, would tell me how much the party has appropriated for the project. In September 2006 Moore (who supports a DNC resolution calling for a move to verified paper voting records by 2008) told me he had a staff of five working with pro bono lawyers in eighteen states. He acknowledged that there was more work ahead. "We're late, but we get it. It's going to take years to fix this system." Now that it has swept the nation, losing not a single seat, many wonder whether the party will ever get around to that work.

In 2006 Democrats picked up blue seats in red states. Dean's fifty-state plan can claim credit for the role its state party staffers played in places in Arizona, Florida, Indiana, Kentucky, and Kansas that have historically voted Republican. Democratic gains in Congress and among the nation's governors were matched by a surge in state legislatures, where more than 275 seats and 10 legislative chambers from Iowa to

Oregon switched overnight from Republican to Democratic hands. With six new Democratic governors, Democrats became the one-party government in fifteen states—including New Hampshire for the first time since 1874, and Colorado for the first time since 1960. No party has controlled that many states since the Republicans achieved that same number after the 1994 election.

In 2004, as one party activist put it to me, "Not only was there no one driving the bus, there was no bus." Dean's Fifty-State Strategy makes a stab at building a bus. Assuming that Dean is permitted to continue his plan, there remains the question of who drives and where do they head.

The turmoil in which the party finds itself today bears striking resemblances to the party's last great crisis, in the civil rights years. Then the question was, could the party of Dixiecrat segregationists reinvent itself to be the party of minority voters, poor voters, women, immigrants, and the working class? Today as then, the Democratic Party stands to gain from any effort to register, protect, and represent the most vulnerable voters. But up to now, the party has never taken that direction. One reason is that the power of the old party machine never did pass to the grassroots activists who had forced the party's transformation in the 1960s. It got bottled up in Washington instead. Student Nonviolent Coordinating Committee (SNCC) organizer Hollis Watkins, who still lives in Mississippi, remembers believing that if black people registered enough they'd be given a seat at the table. "We wanted to believe it, we believed it, but we were naïve," he says today. Black Mississippians formed the Mississippi Freedom Democratic Party to challenge the all-white, prosegregation delegation their state party sent to the Democratic Convention of 1964. LBJ was running for office on his civil rights record; he wasn't planning on confronting white supremacy within the party itself. The segregationist delegation was seated. Fanny Lou Hamer and the Freedom Democrats were shut out. Four years later, the Mississippi state delegation was integrated, but by then front-line activists like Watkins had lost confidence. The DNC of the 1970s, determined to avoid confrontations on the floor of the convention like those of 1964, or those with the peace movement in 1968 and 1972, changed the rules on nominating presidential candidates so as to re-duce the power of state parties and root the selection process in state-wide primaries. State party posts became sinecures, and conventions became dreary propaganda affairs, where the deals are worked out in backrooms in advance. Those in the state parties obey their leaders in D.C. or watch their DNC dollars evaporate.

Money, decision-making power, and influence over policy stayed in Washington, the stomping ground of the party patriarchs, lobbyists, in-tellectuals, and press. Power remained in the suites, not the streets. The party's weakness in the states didn't go unnoticed, but every time the Democratic National Committee appeared to be on the verge of launching a massive voter-registration program, it backed off. In the 1980s Jesse Jackson entered the primaries, and campaign contributors who might have been tapped for the DNC voter-registration effort de-clined to give funds to the party for fear they would end up increasing the Jackson vote.[2] Voting rights expert and George Washington Uni-versity professor Spencer Overton, author of *Stealing Democracy: The New Politics of Voter Suppression,* doesn't understand why Mark Warner, governor of Virginia, who once thought about running for president, didn't do Democrats in his state the favor of re-enfranchising former felons. Florida, Kentucky, and Virginia are alone with Armenia, in all the world, as democracies that ban voting by all ex-felons for life. "He had the opportunity to change the rules and create 300,000 new Demo-cratic voters in a minute, but he didn't do it because he didn't want to be seen to take the felons' side!" exclaims Overton. "But Democrats only hurt themselves by not standing up."

In 2006 African Americans (89 percent of them), Latinos (69 per-cent), and poor people voted even more solidly Democratic. A stunning

60 percent of voters under thirty and 67 percent of voters earning $15,000 or less (and 61 percent of those earning between $15,000 and $30,000) voted blue. How much of the party is ready to take its own side in this fight is a real question. In the summer of 2006, while stumping for Ned Lamont in Connecticut, the Reverend Jesse Jackson told me that "the destiny of the Democratic Party lies in its ability to welcome new voices, especially poor people, people of color, young people, and immigrants." It's not clear just yet how much of the party is committed to that destiny. In Washington, during the midterm election year, Dean's Fifty-State Strategy put a lit match to tensions between the DNC and the committees tasked with electing Democrats to Congress and the Senate. "It's a ten-year plan, not a two-year plan," DNC communications director Karen Finney told me. "There's no denying, we're really challenged." A furious Rahm Emanuel, who headed the Democratic Congressional Campaign Committee in 2006, is said to have stormed out of a meeting with Dean over the governor's refusal to free up resources for candidates' campaigns. "My big thing is, come August, September, October, this is a resources game," Emanuel told *Time*. At the height of the fight Donna Brazile complained bitterly, "You've got Rahm Emanuel beating up on Howard Dean for $60,000. You've got Chuck Schumer [chair of the Democratic Senatorial Campaign Committee] saying 'I need $7 million, not $5 million,' while he has $25 million in his personal PAC. Hillary has $20 million. Bill Nelson, with practically no opposition in Florida, has $15 million. I don't know how much Feinstein has, close to $4 or 5 million. Barack Obama, $4 million. My point is, we have a lot of resources; we just don't share it."

In the spring of 2006, the black caucus of the Louisiana legislature had to fight its own governor, Democrat Kathleen Blanco, and her secretary of state, another Democrat, to help displaced New Orleans residents vote in the municipal elections in their hometown. Advocates for the dispossessed asked the Federal Emergency Management Association (FEMA) to make available a list of relocated people so as to send them voter-registration forms and absentee ballot materials. FEMA refused in the name of protecting "privacy" and "voting integrity." The advocates appealed to the state of Louisiana for out-of-state satellite voting centers. The governor said no. Only when the entire black caucus of the legislature staged a walkout, some of them in tears, accusing the state of blatant racism, did the authorities agree to permit in-state satellite voting centers, for voters in other parts of Louisiana. Tracy Washington, director of the NAACP's Gulf Coast Advocacy Center, had a few words for the governor: "Yo, Kathleen, all these Negroes put your ass in office! How stupid can you be?" Governor Blanco's office did not return my calls. In the media, her argument was based on economics. The state simply did not have the resources, she said, nor were they available from the federal government.

There's good news. On September 27, 2006, Greenwood, Mississippi, elected a new mayor. Just about all the black voters in town and seventy-six whites voted for Sheriel Perkins, the Delta city's first woman mayor and first African American. The legislative black caucus came out to support Sheriel and her husband and campaign manager, Willie Perkins, on Election Day, as did the Magnolia Bar Association, but the two carloads of Mississippi Democratic Party staff didn't return. "We delivered what we promised," campaign director Parmley told me later. The party provided voting lists, conducted robocalls, and sent out a fund-raising letter for the candidate. "I don't remember Election Day monitoring ever being a topic of discussion," he continued. "We knew the local parties were well trained, and the Justice Department was going to be monitoring." Perkins's opponent had RNC lawyers at every black precinct. It took two days to count the provisional and absentee ballots, but Perkins won 3,135 to 2,843. Keelan

Sanders's grandmother was a Mississippi Freedom Party delegate to the 1964 convention. When I asked him why he stuck with the Democratic Party so long, solo, he answered, "Because of my grandmother." Asked about the future, he said, "It's the changing of the guard." Well, maybe. Will those who have dragged the Democrats forward finally be permitted a seat at the party?

It's crunch time for Democrats. An insurgency is in the works. Howard Dean's ascendancy is one example of it, and mini-Dean revolts within the party are taking place all over. Just months after his well-funded 2004 win against a Republican challenger, Governor Mike Easley of North Carolina was rebuffed by his own state Democratic executive committee. The committee rejected his choice for state party chairman in favor of a thirty-four-year-old party activist. The same thing happened in Arkansas: an upstart activist ousted a two-term incumbent for state chair of the Arkansas Democratic Party. In both cases, the victorious candidate accused the party's traditional power structure of being unresponsive to local party activists.

In October 2006, on the eve of his organization's annual convention, Peter MacDowell, president of Progressive Democrats of North Carolina, sounded invigorated. The featured speakers at the convention included a progressive young African American who had just been elected mayor of Asheville. Another was a member of the county board of commissioners, which had just defeated a slate of pro-developer candidates. The keynote speaker was president of the state NAACP, "a very dynamic speaker," MacDowell told me. Why didn't you bring in a national Democratic politician? I asked. Well, MacDowell responded, he'd tried to book Russ Feingold, the Wisconsin senator, but he wasn't available. Democrats who'll stand up for Democratic principles at the national level, he said, are hard to find. "But if we can ever get one with some backbone to stand up, we'll have a great army ready to work for them."

In blue spots all around the country, small *d* democrats with grit are stepping up. Iara Peng at Young People For is training student activists for a lifetime of political engagement. The colleagues of the late Paul Wellstone are conducting Wellstone Action workshops for candidates seeking to work more closely with grassroots organizers across the states.

As the 2007 Congress settles down to work and the fund-raising cycle for the 2008 election starts, young people like Robert "Biko" Baker are looking for change, not just in Congress, but in their lives. A high school soccer coach and scholarship student at the University of California in Los Angeles, Baker put his doctorate on hold in order to come home to Milwaukee to organize voters in 2004. The group he formed (with the help of a dynamic young people's group, the League of Independent Voters) trained a corps of local hip-hop musicians and young performer-poets to walk their blocks. They knocked on doors for four months in a part of town where a young person with a clip-board is a far, *far* more unusual sight than a roadside shrine to a murder victim. (In 2005, 140 people were killed in those streets.) Just days before the 2004 election, the neighborhood was plastered with leaflets warning residents (spuriously, of course) that if they had ever received a parking ticket they couldn't vote. The population that was targeted, mostly black, mostly unemployed, wasn't the typically voting kind; nonetheless, Baker's group registered and turned out fourteen thousand voters that year—three thousand more than John Kerry's margin of victory in Wisconsin. The new activists were elated. "Those kids said it was the best night of their lives." He sent them home that night without telling them Kerry lost.

In the two years since, Baker's group has evolved into a year-round campaign, the Campaign Against Violence, which operates out of an old carpenters' union hall in a part of north Milwaukee they call "little

Beirut." Since 2004 the campaign never stopped working its blocks.
"We're on these blocks and we're from these blocks," said Baker. In 2006
the campaign registered 3,100 new voters and increased turnout in its
precincts by between 5 and, in some places, as much as 50 percent. "In
our target wards we mobilized about 12,000 voters," a tired Baker told
me late November 8. By the end of the season, the campaign was signing up one hundred voters a night, and even high schoolers as young as
fifteen were knocking on doors. "The older folks in the hood couldn't
get over seeing young kids in baggy jeans telling them to vote. They
loved it!"

In Wisconsin, Democrats took control of the state senate 18–15,
gaining four seats. In the legislature they narrowed the gap from 20
seats to 7 seats, knocking out four GOP incumbents. The only big ir-
regularity complaints came from the high turnout. Voting lines were
very long.

"People say young cats aren't serious, but no one wants change
more than these young people," Baker said. For evidence, he points to
one event in the 2004 campaign. When the newspaper reported that the
local county mayor was not planning to print the legally required number of ballots, forty or fifty campaign members walked into the mayor's
office and interrupted a press conference. Having signed up so many
voters, the group wasn't about to see any new registrants turned away.
"I called my people together and said look, we need to mob up and
handle this," William Campbell, president of the black student union
at the local technical college, explained. "And we took care of it." Milwaukee printed the full complement of ballots.

Baker wants to know whether the Democratic Party is finally serious. "We'll find out soon enough," he sighs. "We're here. We're not
going away. So far the party doesn't seem to care." Is the party ready to
"mob up" for the likes of Biko? Or is it not?

EPILOGUE: ☆ Blue Grit in 2008

As the 2008 presidential race heats up, the question at the heart of this book is more keenly felt than ever. Can Democratic people take over the Democratic Party? They're certainly trying. To the party establishment, that's *trying* in both senses of the word.

On November 7, 2006 registered Democrats outnumbered Republicans at the polls for the first time in any midterm election since 1990. Repelled by the record of the Bush administration at home and by the U.S. war and occupation in Iraq, voters elected a Democratic majority in both houses of Congress. As in 2004, Americans didn't just vote. They walked blocks, raised money, monitored polling places, ran for office; they used new media (and old media in new ways), all in an effort to bring about change. Asked in exit polls which was their most pressing issue, 41 percent of all voters and three-quarters of all Democrats identified Iraq. No other issue came close and none came within 10 percentage points of the war.

Almost a year later, not only has the war not ended, but the number of U.S. troops occupying Iraq has increased, and all but a handful of Democrats have voted to extend the conflict by appropriating more money for combat. As for restoring habeas corpus rights to noncitizen detainees, or eliminating military tribunals, or reining in government spies—no luck. In a rush before the August 2007 break, sufficient Democrats joined with Republicans to grant the president even more sweeping spying powers.

Where does that leave Blue Grit America? Almost a year after the November '06 vote, the most vocal callers to Air America Radio were angry. They were especially angry in September, when twenty-one Democratic senators, including supposedly progressive newcomers Jon Tester (D-MT), James Webb (D-VA), and Amy Klobuchar (D-MN), voted to condemn the mass membership group MoveOn after the organization ran a newspaper ad that was critical of the top U.S. general in Iraq. Given the help MoveOn's members have given to Democrats there's no question, liberals were mad about that. But Blue Grit democrats—big and little D—are a heterogeneous bunch. Some are working within the Democratic Party, at the Democratic National Committee, for example, to invigorate the state parties. Others position themselves as a shadow party-in-waiting. Among those are the most influential bloggers, many of the 527 group leaders, and at least some of the Democratic Alliance billionaires. They've moved campaign power off the Party plantation—but you get the feeling that they'd happily join the next Democratic president's cabinet. The most gritty of the blues with grit, however, aren't only interested in pulling off a personnel change in Washington. They'd like that, yes, but they're interested in more, and they understand it won't come quickly.

Blue Gritters have made an impact. You can measure it in time spent on the campaign trail by Democratic candidates. Every contender has added new stops, to attend the Campaign for America's Future-sponsored "Take Back America" conference, for example, or the bloggers' convention "Yearly Kos." At the first "Yearly" shindig, only one declared candidate dropped by (Governor Bill Richardson of New Mexico). In 2007, all but a couple made an appearance, and when Hillary Clinton was tempted to skip the part of the event where she'd be grilled by the conventioneers the resulting brouhaha convinced her to reverse that decision quick.

In the important new early primary states it's hard to find a Blue Grit group that hasn't received a call from a potential presidential candidate, and at the national level, traditional "blue" voters are coming in for new attention. For the first time, the candidates agreed to participate in a live debate on Univision, the nation's largest Spanish speaking television network. The Clinton campaign appointed Dina Titus, who ran for governor in Nevada in 2006, to head up a group called "Women of the West," to stump for women's votes in western states. The candidates fell over themselves to appear gay-friendly in a question and answer session on the LOGO lesbian and gay cable channel (another first). Governor Richardson, Dennis Kucinich, and Michael Gravel showed up for the first ever candidates' debate on reservation land, hosted by INDN's List, a new organization formed to recruit and train Native Americans to run for office. "By 2010 this will be a must-attend event," Howard Dean told me.

It's no surprise that candidates adopt Blue Grit style during primary season. Every candidate wants the kind of influential "grass-top" endorsements that have the power to turn out party faithful to vote. Besides, "the candidates know who's going to be out in the streets for them at the end of the day," quips Jan Gilbert of the Progressive Leadership Alliance of Nevada.

As the '06 election showed, however, even a new Democratic majority in both chambers didn't usher in new power for a new agenda. After all, the newly elected progressives were weak and marginalized. Congressional newcomers Carole Shea-Porter (D-NH) and John Hall (D-NY) came into Washington flush with victory, having scored upset wins running on antiwar platforms with independent, grassroots support. No sooner had they set up their D.C. offices than they came under pressure from the party's leadership to approve new Iraq war spending. Even with a 37 to 29 majority on the House Appropriations Committee—and twelve of those Democrats belonged to the Out of Iraq Caucus—Democrats didn't have the spine to stop war-appropriations bills coming up for a vote and Shea-Porter and Hall voted yea, with two hundred other Democrats.

It would be easy for blues with grit to get discouraged. Some are. But the political shift this book heralds is taking place at a different level. The top of the ticket is not where the action is. Political change, as opposed to personnel change, works from the bottom up and after another year on the road, talking to people about *Blue Grit* I feel more strongly than ever that it's happening.

Just as they cover presidential campaigns as if they were horse races and only the horses matter, so too, the dominant media would have us believe that everything really important that happens in America happens in Washington, D.C. But real change, which is to say, change in the nation's political priorities, happens last, not first, in the nation's capital. The Right understood that. Richard Viguerie, Paul Weyrich, Phyllis Schlafly, et al. didn't pack up their bags and declare victory in 1980, when Ronald Reagan won the White House, or in 1994, when the GOP swept Congress. In power or out of it, the Right invested in infrastructure—in think tanks and media, but most importantly in the states—so as to build up sufficient power and influence to shift attitudes. "The last people we trusted were party leaders," Viguerie told me in an interview in late 2006. "Our job was changing the leaders."

It's not true what so many say today, that the Democratic Party lacks ideas. To the contrary, a battle of ideas is raging. As Connie Baker, a party activist in DuPage County, Illinois, put it to me, at the heart of the matter is what it means to be a party. "Do Democrats even *want* a party or just a small group making decisions as the top?" Over everything from the use of force, to health care, civil rights, trade, urban and rural development, corporate regulation, education, and the way the United States elects its government, the Blue Grit grassroots are head-to-head against the penthouse set. While the Penthouse Party-people and their media allies trumpet the notion that some ideas are just "too extreme" to win in America, the Blue Gritters show it's not the ideas that are too extreme, it's the extremely miserable way the party's leaders handle them.

It's going to be a long, bruising fight. The brute reality is the Penthouse Party set would rather lose elections than loosen their grip on power—and on the party's ideas. The Christine Cegelis race is a case in point. Cegelis opposed the war before it started. She's anti-NAFTA, pro-single-payer health care, and in 2004, with strong grassroots support, she took on arch-conservative Henry Hyde and won 44 percent of the vote despite being massively outspent. In 2006 (Hyde having retired), instead of helping Cegelis to take on the former Tom DeLay aide running for Hyde's seat, DCCC chair Rahm Emanuel went on a candidate-hunt, approaching half a dozen people to run against her until he found Tammy Duckworth, an Iraq war veteran who agreed with Emanuel on trade, on health care, on the war. (She wasn't against the war, only the way the war was fought.) Led by Emanuel, all the prominent Democrats in the country—John Kerry, Hillary Clinton, Barack Obama, Nancy Pelosi—endorsed Duckworth. She outspent Cegelis ten times over, narrowly won the primary, but lost in November, one of the few Democratic defeats of the night. The Duckworth campaign closed up shop leaving nothing behind except a torn up local party without a single Democrat elected in the entire district.

Cegelis would run again, if the state party would support her, but so far they won't. They say that she and her backers are too extreme. "Is it too extreme to want a worker to earn enough to be able to take her kids to a movie once in a while and still afford their dinner? Is it too extreme to believe it's not right to pre-emptively blow people up? If that's too extreme then so be it," says Amy Tauchman, who worked with Baker on Cegelis's campaign. Today, Cegelis, Tauchman, and Baker are active again, in organizations including Turn DuPage Blue and the Greater Chicago Caucus, a grassroots coalition of minority and peace and justice groups they hope will be able to shift the result of elections and the direction of the party. Sometime. Some people just don't give up.

Acknowledgments

If not for the indomitable Elyse Cheney, this book would never have been more than a thought. If not for Ann Godoff, it would never have been published or been called *Blue Grit*. Inigo Thomas helped kick things off. Vanessa Mobley, a gladiator of an editor, created calm out of chaos and insulated me from I'll never know what (but I can guess). My thanks to all of you for having the guts to leap with me into this project. You deserve rowdy applause and many drinks.

The researcher on this project was Eileen Clancy. Thank you. I had additional help from Malav Kanuga, Sarah Goldstein, and Jan Frel. At The Penguin Press, my gratitude goes to Lindsay Whalen, Barbara Campo, and Noirin Lucas, the gentle guides and guardians of these pages.

This book turned out to be like some movements in that more people fed into it than appear out front. I talked to many generous, smart souls who are not named in these pages, but who, I hope, will be able to see the impact of their insights throughout. I thank you for your precious time and thoughts.

Radio is a group endeavor. My thanks go to Hamilton Fish at the Nation Institute and *The Nation* magazine for your partnership. At Air

America Radio, cheers go to Sady Sullivan, who plays music that makes me smile, and to Ed Morgan and Gerald Downer for troubleshooting some adventurous broadcast remotes. Ama Christabel Nsiah-Buadi and Steven Rosenfeld put up with a much too distracted host for far too many months. Thank you for pulling way more than your weight and for keeping *RadioNation* sounding smart.

For magical Marfa, thank you, Patrick Lannan, Martha Jessup, Douglas Humble, and Ray Freese. The Lannan Foundation's writing residency program cheers one up about the state of the world. It is a true gift.

Above all, Elizabeth Streb, whose unique blend of grace and grit ignites my head and heart. Forgive me! I love you.

Notes

INTRODUCTION

1. Peter Beinart, "Block Party," *The New Republic,* November 20, 2006.

CHAPTER 1: WHERE'S THE PARTY?

1. From Marge Piercy, *The Moon Is Always Female* (New York: Alfred A. Knopf, 1980).
2. Mark Preston, "Reid to Enlist K Street," *Roll Call,* January 24, 2005.
3. Michael Tomasky, "Party in Search of a Notion," *American Prospect,* April 4, 2006.
4. Jane McAlevey, "Don't Just Mobilize—Organize," in *Start Making Sense: Turning the Lessons of Election 2004 into Winning Progressive Politics,* eds. Don Hazen and Lakshmi Chaudhry (White River Junction, Vt.: Chelsea Green, 2005), p. 204.
5. Quoted in Oliver Burkeman, "Ruthless Campaign Mastermind Got the Republican Vote Out," *The Guardian,* November 4, 2004.

CHAPTER 2: RED-STATE BLUES

1. Ted Wilson and LaVarr Webb, "Outspoken Rocky Will Be Tough to Beat," *Deseret News,* September 8, 2002, p. AA1.

2. Quoted in John B. Judis and Ruy Teixeira, *The Emerging Democratic Majority* (New York: Scribner, 2002), p. 127.

3. Bob Bernick, "Stance on Same-Sex Marriage Is Likely to Handicap Anderson," *Salt Lake Tribune,* July 5, 1996, p. 2.

4. Rocky Anderson, "'But they didn't win': Politics and Integrity," *Dialogue: A Journal of Mormon Thought,* vol. 31, no. 1 (Spring 1998).

5. Chip Ward, *Canaries on the Rim: Living Downwind in the West* (New York: Verso, 1999), p. 60.

6. Frank E. Moss, *The Water Crisis* (New York: Praeger, 1967); Frank Moss and Val J. Halamandaris, *Too Old, Too Sick, Too Bad: Nursing Homes in America* (Germantown, Md.: Aspen Systems, 1977).

7. David Halberstam, *The Best and the Brightest* (New York: Fawcett Crest, 1972), p. 362.

CHAPTER 3: MONTANA MIRACLE WORKERS

1. Orland J. Singe, "Jim Crow, Indian Style," in *Montana Legacy: Essays on People and Place,* ed. Harry W. Fritz, Mary Murphy, and Robert R. Warmouth Jr. (Helena: Montana Historical Society Press, 2002), p. 276.

CHAPTER 4: DEMOCRATIC DOLLARS

1. Chip Berlet, "Social Movements Need an Infrastructure to Succeed," *Z Magazine,* September 2005; online at http://zmagsite.zmag.org/Sep2005/berlet0905.html.

CHAPTER 5: LEARNING TO LOVE THE CULTURE WARS

1. Nicholas Kristof, "Living Poor, Voting Rich," *New York Times,* November 3, 2004.

2. Randall Rothenberg, *The Neo-Liberals* (New York: Simon & Schuster, 1984), p. 47.

3. Ellen Willis, "Escape from Freedom," *Situations*, vol 1., no 2 (2000).

CHAPTER 6: NOT BY SPIN ALONE

1. Pennington County Democrats website—http://penndemocrats.blogspot .com/2006/07/district-35.html.

2. George Lakoff, *Don't Think of an Elephant!: Know Your Values and Frame the Debate—The Essential Guide for Progressives* (White River Junction, Vt.: Chelsea Green, 2004).

3. Bill Napoli, *NewsHour With Jim Lehrer*, PBS, March 3, 2006.

4. Alan Crawford, *Thunder on the Right: The New Right and the Politics of Resentment* (New York: Pantheon, 1980), p. 198.

CHAPTER 7: MEGAPHONES FOR THE MASSES

1. Quoted in Adam Nagourney and Sheryl Gay Stoltenberg, "Some Democrats Are Sensing Missed Opportunities," *New York Times*, February 8, 2006, p. A1.

2. Ari Melber, "Ned Lamont's Digital Constituency," *The Nation*, August 9, 2006; online at http://www.thenation.com/doc/20060814/melber.

3. Benjamin Wallace-Wells, "Kos Call," *The Washington Monthly*, January/February 2006.

CHAPTER 8: MOBBING UP

1. Quoted in "The New Face of Jim Crow: Voter Suppression in America" (Washington, D.C.: People for the American Way Foundation, August 2006); www.pfaw.org.

2. Karen Paget, "Citizen Organizing: Many Movements, No Majority," *American Prospect*, June 1, 1990.

Index